PCHS Media Center
Grant, Nebraska

INTRODUCING
ISSUES WITH
OPPOSING
VIEWPOINTS®

Religion in Schools

Noël Merino, *Book Editor*

GREENHAVEN PRESS
A part of Gale, Cengage Learning

GALE
CENGAGE Learning·

Detroit • New York • San Francisco • New Haven, Conn • Waterville, Maine • London

Elizabeth Des Chenes, *Managing Editor*

© 2012 Greenhaven Press, a part of Gale, Cengage Learning

Gale and Greenhaven Press are registered trademarks used herein under license.

For more information, contact:
Greenhaven Press
27500 Drake Rd.
Farmington Hills, MI 48331-3535
Or you can visit our Internet site at gale.cengage.com

ALL RIGHTS RESERVED.
No part of this work covered by the copyright herein may be reproduced, transmitted, stored, or used in any form or by any means graphic, electronic, or mechanical, including but not limited to photocopying, recording, scanning, digitizing, taping, Web distribution, information networks, or information storage and retrieval systems, except as permitted under Section 107 or 108 of the 1976 United States Copyright Act, without the prior written permission of the publisher.

For product information and technology assistance, contact us at

Gale Customer Support, 1-800-877-4253
For permission to use material from this text or product, submit all requests online at www.cengage.com/permissions

Further permissions questions can be e-mailed to permissionrequest@cengage.com

Articles in Greenhaven Press anthologies are often edited for length to meet page requirements. In addition, original titles of these works are changed to clearly present the main thesis and to explicitly indicate the author's opinion. Every effort is made to ensure that Greenhaven Press accurately reflects the original intent of the authors. Every effort has been made to trace the owners of copyrighted material.

Cover image © Don Hammond/Design Pics/Getty Images

LIBRARY OF CONGRESS CATALOGING-IN-PUBLICATION DATA

Religion in schools / Noël Merino, book editor.
    p. cm. -- (Introducing issues with opposing viewpoints)
Includes bibliographical references and index.
ISBN 978-0-7377-5685-2 (hardcover)
1. Religion in the public schools--United States. I. Merino, Noël.
LC111.R472 2012
379.280973--dc23

2011039187

Printed in the United States of America
1 2 3 4 5 6 7 16 15 14 13 12

Contents

Chapter 1: Should Religion Be Allowed in Public Schools?

Chapter 2: Should Public Schools Teach Alternatives to Evolution?

Foreword

Indulging in a wide spectrum of ideas, beliefs, and perspectives is a critical cornerstone of democracy. After all, it is often debates over differences of opinion, such as whether to legalize abortion, how to treat prisoners, or when to enact the death penalty, that shape our society and drive it forward. Such diversity of thought is frequently regarded as the hallmark of a healthy and civilized culture. As the Reverend Clifford Schutjer of the First Congregational Church in Mansfield, Ohio, declared in a 2001 sermon, "Surrounding oneself with only like-minded people, restricting what we listen to or read only to what we find agreeable is irresponsible. Refusing to entertain doubts once we make up our minds is a subtle but deadly form of arrogance." With this advice in mind, Introducing Issues with Opposing Viewpoints books aim to open readers' minds to the critically divergent views that comprise our world's most important debates.

Introducing Issues with Opposing Viewpoints simplifies for students the enormous and often overwhelming mass of material now available via print and electronic media. Collected in every volume is an array of opinions that captures the essence of a particular controversy or topic. Introducing Issues with Opposing Viewpoints books embody the spirit of nineteenth-century journalist Charles A. Dana's axiom: "Fight for your opinions, but do not believe that they contain the whole truth, or the only truth." Absorbing such contrasting opinions teaches students to analyze the strength of an argument and compare it to its opposition. From this process readers can inform and strengthen their own opinions, or be exposed to new information that will change their minds. Introducing Issues with Opposing Viewpoints is a mosaic of different voices. The authors are statesmen, pundits, academics, journalists, corporations, and ordinary people who have felt compelled to share their experiences and ideas in a public forum. Their words have been collected from newspapers, journals, books, speeches, interviews, and the Internet, the fastest growing body of opinionated material in the world.

Introducing Issues with Opposing Viewpoints shares many of the well-known features of its critically acclaimed parent series, Opposing Viewpoints. The articles are presented in a pro/con format, allowing readers to absorb divergent perspectives side by side. Active reading questions preface each viewpoint, requiring the student to approach the material thoughtfully and carefully. Useful charts, graphs, and cartoons supplement each article. A thorough introduction provides readers with crucial background on an issue. An annotated bibliography points the reader toward articles, books, and websites that contain additional information on the topic. An appendix of organizations to contact contains a wide variety of charities, nonprofit organizations, political groups, and private enterprises that each hold a position on the issue at hand. Finally, a comprehensive index allows readers to locate content quickly and efficiently.

Introducing Issues with Opposing Viewpoints is also significantly different from Opposing Viewpoints. As the series title implies, its presentation will help introduce students to the concept of opposing viewpoints and learn to use this material to aid in critical writing and debate. The series' four-color, accessible format makes the books attractive and inviting to readers of all levels. In addition, each viewpoint has been carefully edited to maximize a reader's understanding of the content. Short but thorough viewpoints capture the essence of an argument. A substantial, thought-provoking essay question placed at the end of each viewpoint asks the student to further investigate the issues raised in the viewpoint, compare and contrast two authors' arguments, or consider how one might go about forming an opinion on the topic at hand. Each viewpoint contains sidebars that include at-a-glance information and handy statistics. A Facts About section located in the back of the book further supplies students with relevant facts and figures.

Following in the tradition of the Opposing Viewpoints series, Greenhaven Press continues to provide readers with invaluable exposure to the controversial issues that shape our world. As John Stuart Mill once wrote: "The only way in which a human being can make some approach to knowing the whole of a subject is by hearing what can be said about it by persons of every variety of opinion and studying all modes in which it can be looked at by every character of mind. No wise man ever acquired his wisdom in any mode but this." It is to this principle that Introducing Issues with Opposing Viewpoints books are dedicated.

Introduction

"There is a crucial difference between government speech endorsing religion, which the Establishment Clause forbids, and private speech endorsing religion, which the Free Speech and Free Exercise Clauses protect."

—US Supreme Court justice Sandra Day O'Connor, *Board of Education of Westside Community Schools v. Mergens* (1990).

T he First Amendment to the US Constitution guarantees, "Congress shall make no law respecting an establishment of religion, or prohibiting the exercise thereof." The first clause, known as the Establishment Clause, prohibits the government from establishing or endorsing any official religion, requiring that government be neutral toward religion. The second clause, known as the Free Exercise Clause, prohibits the government from barring the exercise of religion by citizens who are religious. Together, these clauses form the foundation of religious freedom in the United States, which simultaneously forbids government from promoting any particular religion while allowing people to practice religion if they so choose. Balancing these two principles in the public sphere is tricky, as neutrality toward religion risks becoming hostility to religion, and accommodation of religion risks becoming endorsement of religion. This tension is particularly evident in the public schools, where social battles over the role of religion continue to play out.

The First Amendment's guarantees of freedom from government establishment of religion and free exercise of religion apply to public schools, as elsewhere in the public sphere. The US Supreme Court's opinion in *Lee v. Weisman* (1992) noted that the public school context was one in which the government must be particularly careful about establishing or endorsing religion: "What to most believers may seem nothing more than a reasonable request that the nonbeliever respect their religious practices, in a school context may appear to the nonbeliever or dissenter to be an attempt to employ the machinery of the State to enforce a religious orthodoxy." Based on the Establishment Clause, the court has concluded over the last few decades that public school officials may not engage in activities that would appear to endorse a particular religion, such as starting the day with a Bible passage or a prayer, posting religious material such as the Ten Commandments, or avoiding the teaching of evolution in order to promote religious theories.

Even though the court has held that public school officials may not sponsor religious activities, the court has recognized that the Free Exercise Clause of the First Amendment protects the rights of students to engage in private religious activity at school. As the court noted in *Board of Education of Westside Community Schools v. Mergens* (1990), "There is a crucial difference between government speech endorsing religion, which the Establishment Clause forbids, and private speech endorsing religion, which the Free Speech and Free Exercise Clauses protect." Thus, as long as student religious activity at school is private, it is protected. The US Department of Education clarifies that "students may read their Bibles or other scriptures, say grace before meals, and pray or study religious materials with fellow students during recess, the lunch hour, or other noninstructional time to the same extent that they may engage in nonreligious activities." However, the Department of Education also notes that student religious expression, as with other privately initiated student expression, may be limited when students are engaged in school activities and instruction, cautioning that "the Constitution mandates neutrality rather than hostility toward privately initiated religious expression."[1]

One particularly contentious issue regarding religion in public schools is that of prayer. In 1962 the Supreme Court ruled that even a voluntary, nondenominational school prayer led by a public school official violated the Establishment Clause of the First Amendment. Outside of the classroom, the court has also concluded that some prayers are unconstitutional. In 1992 the court ruled that it is a violation of the Establishment Clause to allow prayers led by religious authorities at public school graduation ceremonies. However, the court noted in *Santa Fe Independent School District v. Doe* (2000), that "nothing in the Constitution as interpreted by this Court prohibits any public school student from voluntarily praying at any time before, during, or after the schoolday." On the one hand, school-led prayer violates the Establishment Clause but, on the other hand, student-led prayer is protected by the Constitution.

The prohibition on school-led prayer and the protection of student-led prayer collide on the issue of student-led graduation prayer. The US Supreme Court has not addressed this issue as of the end of 2011, and opinions differ on what kind of protection should be given to the religious speech of students who speak at public school graduations. The circuit courts have come to contradictory findings, with the Fifth Circuit determining that the student-led graduation prayer does not violate the Constitution and the Ninth Circuit finding that it does. The Rutherford Institute agrees with the Fifth Circuit, arguing that "students who have been selected to speak at a graduation ceremony may voluntarily pray as long as the ceremony is planned and organized by the student body independent of school officials."[2] The American Civil Liberties Union disagrees, claiming that "when public schools reserve time at a graduation ceremony for prayers, they violate the Constitution by putting the power, prestige and endorsement of the state behind whatever prayer is offered, no matter who offers it."[3]

The debate about school prayer both in and out of the classroom is likely to continue. As history shows, even once the Supreme Court decides the issue, not everyone agrees with the outcome. For example, the issues of prayer, Bible study, and the teaching of creationism within the classroom are still debated in society despite the fact that the court has reached conclusions on these issues. These matters of disagreement regarding the role of religion in US public schools are among the many fascinating debates explored in *Introducing Issues with Opposing Viewpoints: Religion in Schools.*

Notes

1. US Department of Education, "Guidance on Constitutionally Protected Prayer in Public Elementary and Secondary Schools," February 7, 2003. www2.ed.gov/policy/gen/guid/religionand schools/prayer_guidance.html.
2. Rutherford Institute, "The Ten Commandments of Prayer and Religious Expression at Graduation Ceremonies," 2007. www .rutherford.org/pdf/graduationprayerguidelines.pdf.
3. American Civil Liberties Union, "The Establishment Clause and Public Schools," *ACLU Legal Bulletin*, March 11, 2002. www.aclu .org/religion-belief/establishment-clause-and-schools-legal-bulletin.

Chapter 1

Should Religion Be Allowed in Public Schools?

Whether religion should be allowed in public schools has been a hotly debated issue for decades.

Viewpoint

1

Public Schools Must Not Promote nor Inhibit Religion

Charles C. Haynes and Oliver Thomas

"The First Amendment does not mandate that public schools be religion-free zones."

In the following viewpoint Charles C. Haynes and Oliver Thomas argue that there is new consensus on the role of religion in public schools. Finding a third way between the extremes of religious inculcation and the absence of religion, Haynes and Thomas contend that it is both constitutional and just for schools to protect the religious liberty of students as long as schools do not engage in indoctrination. Charles C. Haynes is senior scholar at the First Amendment Center and author of *First Freedoms: A Documentary History of First Amendment Rights in America.* Oliver Thomas is executive director of the Niswonger Foundation in eastern Tennessee, a lawyer, and a minister.

Charles C. Haynes and Oliver Thomas, "From Battleground to Common Ground," *Finding Common Ground: A First Amendment Guide to Religion and Public Schools,* First Amendment Center, 2007. © 2007 First Amendment Center. Reproduced by permission.

AS YOU READ, CONSIDER THE FOLLOWING QUESTIONS:
1. The authors point to what feature of America that stands out among developed countries?
2. Haynes and Thomas contend that a new consensus on religion in public schools began to emerge after what events in the mid-1980s?
3. According to the authors, what model is at the other end of the spectrum from the "sacred public school" model?

More than 200 years after their enactment, the first 16 words of the Bill of Rights undergird the boldest and most successful experiment in religious freedom in human history. Despite periodic outbreaks of nativism, anti-Semitism and religious conflict, Americans can be justly proud that we begin the new century as one nation of many peoples and faiths.

The First Amendment

The challenge for 21st-century America is not only to sustain this extraordinary arrangement, but to expand the principles of religious liberty more fairly and justly to each and every citizen. This is no small task. Today the United States is the most religiously diverse society on Earth and, among developed countries, the most religious. But exploding religious pluralism combined with bitter culture wars are making our public square an increasingly crowded and often hostile arena.

Nowhere is it more important—or more difficult—to address our growing ideological and religious diversity than in the public schools. Not only are our schools a key battleground in the culture wars, they are the principal institution charged with enabling Americans to live with our deepest differences. If we fail in our schools to teach and model the rights and responsibilities that flow from the First Amendment, then surely we endanger the future of our daring experiment in religious liberty. . . .

The key is for all sides to step back from the debate and to give fresh consideration to the democratic first principles that bind us together as a people. Then, in light of our shared civic commitments, we can work for policies and practices in public education that best protect the conscience of every student and parent in our schools.

A New Consensus on Religion in Schools

Here is the good news: Although underreported by the media and still unknown to many school leaders, a new model has emerged for addressing religion and religious liberty in public schools. . . .

The measure of just how much consensus we now have was highlighted in early 2000 when every public-school principal in the United States received a packet of comprehensive religious liberty guidelines from President [Bill] Clinton and the U.S. Department of Education. For the first time in American history, all administrators were given the closest thing possible to a legal safe harbor for addressing perennial conflicts over religion in the schools.

This new consensus on religion in public schools began to emerge as a response to the textbook trials in Alabama and Tennessee in the mid-1980s. Although the constitutional questions were quite different, both cases called attention to the fact that the public-school curriculum largely ignored religious ways of understanding the world. The educational issues raised by the trials were reinforced by several textbook studies. The liberal People for the American Way reached much the same conclusion as the conservative Paul Vitz: Public-school texts included little or nothing about religion.

FAST FACT

The First Amendment to the US Constitution guarantees that "Congress shall make no law respecting the establishment of religion, or prohibiting the free exercise thereof."

In the wake of these trials and studies, we convened leading educational and religious organizations in an effort to find common ground on the question of religion in the curriculum. Groups ranging from the National Association for Evangelicals to the Association for Supervision and Curriculum Development agreed that ignoring religion was neither educationally sound nor consistent with the First Amendment. We were convinced that we can (and must) do better in public education.

Self-Identification of US Adult Population by Religious Tradition, 2008

Religious Tradition	2008 Estimate	2008 Percentage
Catholic	57,199,000	25.1
Baptist	36,148,000	15.8
Mainline Christian	29,375,000	12.9
Methodist	11,366,000	5.0
Lutheran	8,674,000	3.8
Presbyterian	4,723,000	2.1
Episcopalian/Anglican	2,405,000	1.1
United Church of Christ	736,000	0.3
Christian Generic	32,411,000	14.2
Christian Unspecified	16,834,000	7.4
Non-Denom. Christian	8,032,000	3.5
Protestant Unspecified	5,187,000	2.3
Evangelical/Born Again	2,154,000	0.9
Pentecostal/Charismatic	7,948,000	3.5
Pentecostal Unspecified	5,416,000	2.4
Assemblies of God	810,000	0.4
Church of God	663,000	0.3
Protestant Denominations	7,131,000	3.1
Churches of Christ	1,921,000	0.8
Jehovah's Witnesses	1,914,000	0.8
Seventh Day Adventist	938,000	0.4
Mormon/Latter Day Saints	3,158,000	1.4
Jewish*	2,680,000	1.2
Eastern Religions	1,961,000	0.9
Buddhist	1,189,000	0.5
Muslim	1,349,000	0.6
New Religious Movements & Other Religions	2,804,000	1.2
None/No Religion	34,169,000	15.0
Agnostic	1,985,000	0.9
Atheist	1,621,000	0.7
Don't Know/Refused	11,815,000	5.2
Total	228,182,000	100

*This refers to Jews only by religion and not to the total Jewish ethnic population

Taken from: Barry A. Kasmin and Ariela Keysar, American Religious Identification Survey (ARIS 2008), Trinity College, March 2009.

After a year and a half of discussion and debate, we reached agreement on our first set of guidelines, "Religion in the Public School Curriculum: Questions and Answers." Four months later we forged a second agreement, "Religious Holidays in the Public Schools: Questions and Answers." This was soon followed by a third statement providing consensus guidelines for implementing the Equal Access Act. After a long history of shouting past one another, we had begun to find common ground.

Beyond Two Failed Models

These agreements of the late 1980s and early 1990s were important first steps in articulating a civic framework that enables school and communities to move beyond culture-war debates that are often dominated by extremes.

On one end of the spectrum are those who advocate what might be called the "sacred public school," where one religion (theirs) is preferred in school policies and practices. Characteristic of the early history of public education, this approach still survives in some parts of the United States, particularly the rural South. From the "Bible wars" of the 19th century to current fights over posting the Ten Commandments in classrooms, attempts to impose religion in schools have fueled countless lawsuits and bitter fights in communities throughout the nation. Not only is this model unconstitutional, it is also unjust.

In recent decades, however, some on the other end of the spectrum have pushed for a "naked public school," where religion is excluded in the name of the Establishment clause of the First Amendment. The influence of this mistaken view of the First Amendment is apparent in the virtual silence about religion in most of the curriculum and the confusion among many school leaders about the religious-liberty rights of students. But the First Amendment does not mandate that public schools be religion-free zones. This approach is also unjust and, when the rights of students are violated, unconstitutional.

The Civil Public School

The process of finding consensus during the past decade has yielded a third model—what might be called a "civil public school." . . .

Some contend that it is constitutionally legal for schools to protect the religious liberty of students, as long as religion is neither inhibited nor indoctrinated.

Twenty-four major religious and educational organizations define religious liberty in public schools this way:

Public schools may not inculcate nor inhibit religion. They must be places where religion and religious conviction are treated with fairness and respect.

Public schools uphold the First Amendment when they protect the religious-liberty rights of students of all faiths or none. Schools demonstrate fairness when they ensure that the curriculum includes study *about* religion, where appropriate, as an important part of a complete education.

These four sentences restate the civic framework of the religious-liberty clauses of the First Amendment—our constitutional commitment to "no establishment" and "free exercise"—as they apply to public education. They describe what schools might look like if we finally lived up to the promise of religious liberty. Rather than simply telling public schools what they may not do, the statement calls for protecting student religious expression and including religious perspectives in the curriculum, while simultaneously rejecting government endorsement or promotion of religion.

EVALUATING THE AUTHOR'S ARGUMENTS:

In this viewpoint Charles C. Haynes and Oliver Thomas claim that, within certain limitations, schools may teach about religion. What kinds of things do you think they have in mind that would be acceptable within their "civil public school" model?

Viewpoint

2

Public Schools Have Been Overly Sanitized of Religion

"In an attempt to avoid offending anyone, America's public schools have increasingly adopted a zero-tolerance attitude toward religious expression."

John W. Whitehead

In the following viewpoint John W. Whitehead argues that religion has been unreasonably excluded from public schools. Whitehead contends that in recent years students have been censored when they engage in any expression at school that is remotely religious. He recounts a 2009 court ruling to illustrate his view, arguing that the schools and the courts have gone too far in excluding religion. Whitehead concludes that such a zero-tolerance view toward religion at school threatens to remove all culture from education and undermine key American freedoms. Whitehead is an attorney and author and president of the Rutherford Institute.

John W. Whitehead, "The Shaming of Religion," *Liberty,* January–February 2010. Reproduced by permission.

AS YOU READ, CONSIDER THE FOLLOWING QUESTIONS:
1. According to Whitehead, an antireligion campaign has resulted in Christians being subjected to what?
2. What Ninth Circuit Court of Appeals ruling does the author point to as evidence of the denial of students' rights?
3. Whitehead claims that what three authors are at risk of being censored if all religious content is removed from the schools?

Religion and religious expression have been objects of censorship in the public schools for quite some time. However, the intolerance of anything related to religion has taken a turn for the absurd in recent years.

The Censorship of Religion

Much of the credit for this state of affairs can be chalked up to those who have been relentlessly working to drive religion from public life in America. John Leo, a former contributing editor at *U.S. News & World Report*, paints a particularly grim picture. Written in 2002, his article was an eerie foreshadowing of our current state of affairs:

> History textbooks have been scrubbed clean of religious references and holidays scrubbed of all religious references and symbols. Some intellectuals now contend that arguments by religious people should be out of bounds in public debate, unless, of course, they agree with the elites.

> In schools the anti-religion campaign is often hysterical. When schoolchildren are invited to write about any historical figure, this usually means they can pick [Joseph] Stalin or Jeffrey Dahmer, but not Jesus or Luther, because religion is reflexively considered dangerous in schools and loathsome historical villains aren't. Similarly, a moment of silence in the schools is wildly controversial because some children might use it to pray silently on public property. Oh, the horror. The overall message is that religion is backward, dangerous, and toxic.

Unfortunately, things have gotten only worse since John Leo wrote those words. As we have seen all too clearly, Christians of all ages are increasingly finding themselves subjected to censorship and discrimination.

A plea for help from Kathryn, a parent in Colorado, is a perfect example of what's happening in America's public schools. Kathryn's son, Wade, is in the fourth grade. His class was given a "Hero" assignment, which required each student to pick a hero, research the person, and write an essay. The student would then dress up and portray the chosen hero as part of a "live wax museum" and give an oral report in front of the class.

When 9-year-old Wade chose Jesus Christ as his hero, school officials immediately insisted that he pick another hero. After Kathryn and her husband objected, the school proposed a compromise: Wade could write the essay on Jesus. He could even dress up like Jesus for the "wax museum." However, he would have to present his oral report to his teacher in private, with no one else present, rather than in front of the classroom like the other students. The message to young Wade, of course, was twofold: first, Jesus Christ is not a worthy hero, and second, Jesus is someone to be ashamed of and kept hidden from public view.

This is not an isolated incident. I have been contacted by a number of parents whose children are being subjected to the same kind of treatment in the schools. For instance, a third grader at an elementary school in Las Vegas, Nevada, was asked to write in her journal what she liked most about the month of December. When the little girl wrote that she liked the month of December because "it's Jesus' birthday and people get to celebrate it," her teacher tapped her on the shoulder and told her that she was not allowed to write about religion in school. And a teacher in a Pennsylvania public school was told that she could not post a picture of the Statue of Liberty in her classroom because it has the words "God Bless America" at the bottom.

It makes no difference that the material in question does not proselytize, or, as we have seen, that it was presented to people who by and large do not know that it was religious, or even that it is not meant to be religious. What matters is what *school officials* consider to be religious.

Copyright 2007 by Mike Lester and CagleCartoons.com. All rights reserved.

A Recent Court Ruling

A ruling by the U.S. Court of Appeals for the Ninth Circuit in *Nurre v. Whitehead* [2009], which affirms the right of school administrators to censor material that has the remotest connection to religion, illustrates exactly how outlandish things have become.

At Henry M. Jackson High School in Snohomish County, Washington, the senior members of the woodwind ensemble, the top performing instrumental group, traditionally select a piece each year to perform during graduation ceremonies. Having performed Franz Biebl's "Ave Maria" at a public concert in 2004, the seniors in the wind ensemble unanimously chose to perform it again at their graduation ceremony on June 17, 2006, because they felt its aesthetic beauty and peacefulness would be appropriate for the tone of the ceremony.

As Kathryn Nurre, a member of the ensemble, explained, "It's the kind of piece that can make your graduation memorable because we actually learned to play it really well. And we wanted to play something that we enjoyed playing."

The student musicians proposed to perform Biebl's piece instrumentally: no lyrics or words would be sung or said, nor did the senior members intend that any lyrics would be printed in ceremony programs or otherwise distributed to members of the audience.

However, despite the absence of lyrics, the school superintendent, Carol Whitehead, refused to allow the ensemble to perform "Ave Maria" at their graduation ceremony because she believed the piece to be religious in nature.

Ironically, the superintendent reportedly didn't even know that the words "Ave Maria" are Latin for "Hail Mary." Nevertheless, determined to avoid offense, despite the fact that this Biebl version of "Ave Maria" is not one that most people would even recognize, the superintendent banned it.

The Right of Free Speech

Believing that school authorities had violated her right of free speech, Nurre turned to us at The Rutherford Institute. We filed a First Amendment lawsuit against the school in federal district court in June 2006. A year later, a federal district court ruled that the school's actions were "reasonable" in trying to avoid offending anyone.

> **FAST FACT**
>
> In March 2010, the US Supreme Court refused to review the opinion of the Ninth Circuit Court of Appeals in *Nurre v. Whitehead* (2009) allowing the prohibition of a religious musical piece at a public school graduation.

In a 2–1 ruling that was handed down in September 2009, the Ninth Circuit Court of Appeals concurred. According to the court, school authorities can deny students' rights to free speech just to keep some of those attending graduation from being offended.

However, in a dissent that is notable for its lucidity, Judge Milan D. Smith insisted that Nurre's right to free speech had been unreasonably violated. "In prohibiting Nurre and her classmates from playing their selected piece of music, the school district misjudged the establishment clause's requirements and, in so doing, violated Nurre's First Amendment rights," observed Smith. He continued:

> I am concerned that, if the majority's reasoning on this issue becomes widely adopted, the practical effect will be for public school administrators to chill—or even kill—musical and artis-

tic presentations by their students in school-sponsored limited public fora where those presentations contain any trace of religious inspiration, for fear of criticism by a member of the public, however extreme that person's views may be.

The First Amendment neither requires nor condones such a result. The taking of such unnecessary measures by school administrators will only foster the increasingly sterile and hypersensitive way in which students may express themselves in such fora, and hasten the retrogression of our young into a nation of Philistines, who have little or no understanding of our civic and cultural heritage.

A Cultural Wasteland

In an attempt to avoid offending anyone, America's public schools have increasingly adopted a zero-tolerance attitude toward religious expression. The courts have not helped, allowing schools the discretion to let an offended minority control a cowed majority. Such politically correct thinking has resulted in a host of inane actions, from the Easter Bunny being renamed "Peter Rabbit" to Christmas concerts being dubbed "Winter" concerts, and some schools even outlaw the colors red and green, saying they're Christmas colors. And now, simply because someone is offended by the title, students cannot play music that has no words and is performed with no religious intent.

What school officials and the courts fail to understand is that by agreeing to sanitize the schools of anything remotely related to religion, they will not only be silencing an entire segment of the population, but will also be contributing to a cultural wasteland bereft of a rich heritage of Western art, music, and literature—all of which, at one time or another, has been greatly influenced by religion.

Where do our children learn about culture, things such as fine art, classical music, great literature, and anything else that really has substance? They surely don't find true culture in strip malls, video games, designer clothing, or movie theaters. Unless their parents make an effort to teach them about the traditions of Western culture, children hardly ever encounter anything more complex than a comic book unless schools teach them about this history.

Religion is such an innate part of American culture that it would be impossible to create a strictly secular course of study for students.

For example, if someone complains about Michelangelo's art because it was so often themed on Christianity, does this mean that we are supposed to have art history books without the Sistine Chapel? What about other masterpieces such as Da Vinci's *Last Supper*? For that matter, what about great writers such as Charles Dickens, Alexandre Dumas, or Edgar Allan Poe?

Some of Western civilization's greatest music was inspired by religion or created for a religious purpose, composed by such maestros as J.S. Bach, Wolfgang Mozart, and Joseph Haydn. Even contemporary artists could find their music banned in schools under such a rubric. For example, the Beatles are visited by Mother Mary in "Let It Be"; Led Zeppelin writes of a "Stairway to Heaven"; and even Jon Bon Jovi sings about "Livin' on a Prayer." Such a course of action would reduce American culture and arts education to a sterile wasteland.

A Matter of Personal Taste

Just as with religion, art has always been a matter of personal experience. Each person brings their own experiences and interpretations to art, rendering it nearly impossible to establish a litmus test for what constitutes "religious art" as opposed to secular art.

Anyone who has ever appreciated a book, painting, symphony, or even a newspaper article, movie, or television show should be repulsed at the idea of government officials dictating what art is—and, more important, what it is not. Anyone who has ever appreciated even a comic book should cringe at the thought of letting the government control it.

This brings us back to the Ninth Circuit's ruling in *Nurre*. We are witnessing the emergence of an unstated yet court-sanctioned right, one that makes no appearance in the Constitution and yet seems to trump the First Amendment at every turn: the right not to be offended. Yet there is no way to completely avoid giving offense. At some time or other, someone is going to take offense at something someone else says or does. It's inevitable.

Each time we allow political correctness to triumph over our constitutional freedoms and basic common sense, we are complicit in undermining the freedoms on which this nation was built. And, in a case such as that of *Nurre v. Whitehead*, we will destroy our culture as well.

EVALUATING THE AUTHOR'S ARGUMENTS:

In this viewpoint John W. Whitehead contends that the right to religious expression is being censored in public schools. How does his position compare with that of Charles C. Haynes and Oliver Thomas, authors of the previous viewpoint?

PCHS Media Center
Grant, Nebraska

Viewpoint

3

Public Schools Should Teach About Different Religions

"Courses in world religions should be mandatory for all public school students."

Michael Tracey

In the following viewpoint Michael Tracey contends that there needs to be more religion in schools. Tracey argues that a recent study shows Americans are ignorant about religions, including their own. He claims that the removal of school prayer from public schools in the 1960s was needed but that the removal of all religion from schools went too far. He proposes that schools teach mandatory classes on world religions, with an emphasis on Christianity. Tracey claims such classes would not endorse religion but would educate students on various religions. Tracey is a writer based in New Jersey.

AS YOU READ, CONSIDER THE FOLLOWING QUESTIONS:
1. According to Tracey, what percentage of Americans can name the four gospels of the Bible?
2. In what two years did the US Supreme Court issue rulings that banned school prayer, according to the author?
3. Which two groups does Tracey say are the most knowledgeable about religion?

Michael Tracey, "Put Religion Back in Public Schools," *Nation,* September 29, 2010. Reproduced by permission.

P ew Research's study released this week [September 28, 2010] detailing the abysmal religious literacy demonstrated by most Americans is disturbing, but not at all surprising. The smear campaign waged against Muslims over the past few months has been a painful reminder of how—especially in a country where gross ignorance of religion is the norm—opportunistic blowhards can easily manipulate matters of alleged supernatural significance. With vast majorities unable to correctly answer even the most basic questions about Islam, for example, is it any wonder that an innocuous Islamic center in Lower Manhattan [near the site of the former twin towers] could spur so much misinformation and hysteria?

American Ignorance of Religion

The grating irony in these sorts of studies, of course, is that despite our illiteracy, America also happens to be the most pious of all major Western democracies. We are constantly hearing about the crucial electoral role of Evangelical Christians, the degree to which politicians are placating their fundamentalist base, and whether gay marriage really does spell the end of civilization. Yet when actually pressed

A Pew study on religion reported that many Catholics do not realize that the wafers used in the ritual of Holy Communion are meant literally to transubstantiate into the flesh of Christ.

Religious Knowledge in the United States

At least two-thirds know:	Percent
An atheist is someone who does not believe in God.	85
Moses was the Bible figure who led the exodus from Egypt.	72
Jesus was born in Bethlehem.	71
Most people in Pakistan are Muslim.	68
About half know:	**Percent**
The golden rule is not one of the Ten Commandments.	55
The Koran is the Islamic holy book.	54
The Dalai Lama is Buddhist.	47
The Jewish Sabbath begins on Friday.	45
Less than a third know:	**Percent**
Most people in Indonesia are Muslim.	27
Only Protestants (not Catholics) traditionally teach that salvation comes through faith alone.	16

Taken from: Pew Research Center's Forum on Religion & Public Life, May 19–June 6, 2010.

about what they believe—even about their own religion's central tenets—a great many Americans simply draw [a] blank.

For one, according to Pew, Catholics do not generally understand that the communal wafers they consume on Sunday mornings are supposed to literally transubstantiate into the flesh of Christ. Only 45 percent of all respondents—the vast majority of whom must have been Christians—can name the four Gospels, and just over half are aware of which religion reveres the Koran.

So what's the proper recourse? Consider this: Pew asked whether public school teachers may legally read from the Bible "as an example of literature." Most respondents answered incorrectly, presumably taking this to represent a violation of the separation of church and state. But, thankfully, that cherished Jeffersonian ideal mandates no such prohibition—it merely proscribes governmental sanction of any particular belief-set. Misconceptions like this one have created the impression that issues of religion are not to enter the public domain; that religion is instead to remain an intensely private matter, untouched by the cultural checks and balances applied to most every other area of human inquiry. Thus, because odious beliefs and distortions are so rarely subjected to meaningful scrutiny, they have been allowed to thrive—festering with a dangerous false sense of constitutionally afforded immunity.

What we need, then, is more religion in schools.

The Banishment of Religion

This remedy may seem counter-intuitive, as the removal of coerced prayer and other forms of religious endorsement from the public school system was, after all, one of the twentieth century's hallmark progressive achievements. But in banishing the promotion of one theology over another, the Warren Court [US Supreme Court from 1953 to 1969, under Chief Justice Earl Warren] certainly did not in turn banish the whole of religion from the academic arena. Rather, when it issued a pair of rulings in 1962 and 1963 outlawing school prayer, the Court merely codified the increasingly popular notion that space in the public sphere should be made for those who do not affirm the majority's belief in Christian creeds. And because prayer itself bore such a heavily Protestant connotation, the Court's only feasible option was to insist that schools be strictly secular—a powerful blow to Christianity's previously unshakable cultural hegemony.

The rulings thus represented an acknowledgement that in postwar America, believers in dissonant and often mutually irreconcilable religious principles were regularly interacting with one another; the newly available automobile allowed the faithful to finally exit their insular bubbles of religious conformity and experience, advancements in communications technology exposed people to doctrines that contradicted their own, new immigration patterns shook up the ecumenical status quo, and so forth. In short, the great engine of pluralism was gathering steam, and the Warren Court decisions reflected this new reality.

> **FAST FACT**
>
> In *Engel v. Vitale* (1962), the US Supreme Court banned official school prayer, and in *Abington Township School District v. Schempp* (1963), the court banned school-sponsored Bible reading.

But as critical as those rulings were to our societal embrace of religious diversity, they also indirectly brought about a pernicious side effect. Religion was largely excised from public curricula out of concern for sensitivity or respect, and we see subsequent embarrassing ignorance manifested in the many insufferable (and preventable) controversies *du jour* [of the day].

The Need for Religion Classes

My proposal: courses in world religions should be mandatory for all public school students, with a focus on Christianity as the most prevalent domestic faith. These courses would examine the philosophical and sociological features of religion, without teachers' needing to fear that such lessons will be construed as an endorsement or denunciation of any particular doctrine. Within reason, their ability to teach freely and honestly must be unhindered.

It is patently unacceptable for so many to know so little about what has been by some accounts the prime mover of world history. The only solution is to shift our educational priorities. In learning more about religion, students will also hopefully recognize that the decision to assign oneself a religious faith is not to be taken lightly, as it bears profound metaphysical, social and even political implications. With any luck, they will also glean that the study of religion is incredibly interesting and fulfilling.

For those wary that an influx of such study will increase actual rates of dogmatic belief, consider one of Pew's most critical findings: self-described atheists and agnostics are actually the most knowledgeable about religion, far outpacing Christians of all stripes. The more we learn about the actual doctrines, then, the less likely we are to adopt them as our own—and, with any luck, the less likely we are to unfairly demonize others. After all, if [conservative politicians] Sarah Palin and Newt Gingrich learned about Islam from [modernizing Islam cleric Mohammed] Al Ghazali instead of [Islamaphobic website] JihadWatch.com, we might've avoided a lot of recent nonsense.

EVALUATING THE AUTHOR'S ARGUMENTS:

In this viewpoint Michael Tracey argues that religion should be studied in public schools, with an emphasis on Christianity. Give one objection to this idea that there should be an emphasis on Christianity.

Public Schools Are Not Equipped to Teach About Different Religions

Susan Jacoby

"When we talk about "mandatory" public school courses dealing with religion, we are really indulging in the fantasy that public schools can do a job that parents and churches are failing to do."

In the following viewpoint Susan Jacoby contends that although she believes Americans should know more about religion, she denies that public schools are the place to teach about religion. Jacoby worries about Americans' ignorance concerning world religions but claims that the broader cultural illiteracy shows that schools already do a poor job with existing curriculum. Adding religion to the mix in public schools, Jacoby argues, is unrealistic given the current culture that is both highly religious and highly ignorant.

Jacoby writes "The Spirited Atheist" column for the *On Faith* blogging network at the *Washington Post* and is author of *Freethinkers: A History of American Secularism.*

Susan Jacoby, "Know-Nothing Nation: Flunking Religion Too," *Washington Post,* March 7, 2007. Reproduced by permission of Georges Borchardt on behalf of the author.

AS YOU READ, CONSIDER THE FOLLOWING QUESTIONS:
1. The author claims that approximately what fraction of Americans can name the first book of the Bible?
2. Jacoby worries about teaching religion in public school because she says there is too fine a line between teaching and what?
3. Three-quarters of Americans wrongly believe the Bible says what, according to Jacoby?

The United States is the most religious nation in the developed world, if religion is measured by churchgoing (or, to be more precise, by the claim that we go to church) and by belief in all things supernatural. Americans are also the most religiously ignorant people in the Western world. Call it blind faith.

American Religious Ignorance

The depth of this religious ignorance is the subject of an important new book, *Religious Literacy*, by Stephen Prothero. Some of Prothero's statistics, based on reliable public opinion polls, are truly astonishing and depressing to anyone—religious or secular—who cares about our common culture. Fewer than half of Americans can name Genesis as the first book of the Bible. Only about half can name even one of the four gospels. One of the more surprising findings is that evangelicals are only marginally more knowledgeable about Christianity than other Americans.

Predictably, we are even more ignorant about Islam and various eastern religions than we are about Christianity and Judaism.

The Need for More Religious Knowledge

I want Americans to know more about religion (as opposed to believing in religion) for two distinct reasons.

First, anyone who hasn't read the Bible lacks one of the most important keys to western literature and culture. I feel sorry for everyone who hasn't read the King James version of the Bible, with its boundless store of allusions and metaphors that do not require faith to be appreciated for their beauty and psychological insight into the best and the worst of human existence.

And the importance of understanding the role of various religions in history—in our own nation and around the world—ought to be obvious at a time when we have gotten ourselves involved in a conflict that is, in part, a civil war between groups of Muslims arguing over which of them is the true heir of the prophet Mohammad (and over political power, of course).

As a freethinker and an atheist, my second reason for wanting Americans to know more about religion is that knowledge fosters skepticism about faith—and I believe that our country needs

The author says that the most religious country in the developed world is the United States, yet much of the population has scant knowledge about the Bible.

much more skepticism and much less faith. If Americans actually read about the actions of a capricious God—his treatment of poor Job, his slaughter of the Egyptian first-born on behalf of Jews, his slaughter of the innocents while sparing Jesus—they might think about whether they want to go on praying to such a heartless and unreliable being. Thank you, Mr. [Johannes] Gutenberg [printer of the famous Gutenberg Bible in the 1450s].

FAST FACT

A recent poll found that 48 percent of religious Americans seldom or never read books (other than Scripture) about their own religion, and 70 percent say they seldom or never read books about other religions.

I regard American religious illiteracy as simply one more manifestation of a broader cultural illiteracy, evinced by our equally deficient knowledge of American and world history. Furthermore, American high school students consistently rank near the bottom in international tests designed to compare the scientific knowledge of teenagers.

An Unreasonable Suggestion

We are doing a poor job of teaching our children what they need to know about history, literature, science, and mathematics. Why should we think that public schools can do a better job of teaching religious history?

Prothero suggests that teachers, parents, and school administrators get together and devise a course about religion to be taught at the high school level. This might work in the best of all possible worlds—a multicultural, educated community that pays its teachers high salaries and is willing to foot the bill for the additional training they would surely need to do justice to such a course. But what sort of curriculum agreement could be reached in communities where teachers are too intimidated by fundamentalist parents to use the word "evolution" in biology classes?

There is no Constitutional bar to teaching about religion, as distinct from indoctrinating children in particular religious beliefs. But that is really beside the point, because the line between teaching and preaching is too fine for the average public school. To take just one straightforward example, Christians believe that Jesus was the Messiah—the fulfillment of Old Testament prophecy—and Jews believe that Jesus was, well, just another Jew. An interesting Jew, perhaps a Jewish prophet, but a Jewish man and no more. I would love to hear the average high school teacher explain this "straight-forward" fact of religious history, and its relationship to historical anti-Semitism, to a class of 16-year-olds.

Furthermore, if we are going to teach the history of religion, we will also have to teach the history of secularism—something totally neglected now in public school American history classes. In a history of religion class, a teacher would have to explain why the founders deliberately left the word "God" out of the Constitution and why there was so much debate about that omission at the time. I'd be happy to have this bit of history included in a public school class, but I'll bet some other parents would storm the principal's office.

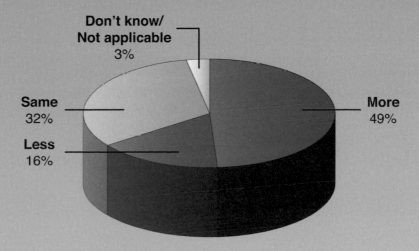

Americans' Views on Religion in Schools

"Would you like to see religious and spiritual values have more influence in the schools than they do now, less influence, or about the same influence as they do now?"

Don't know/ Not applicable 3%

Same 32%

Less 16%

More 49%

Taken from: CBS News poll, *Teaching the Bible*, April 6–9, 2006.

The Real Problem of Ignorance

When we talk about "mandatory" public school courses dealing with religion, we are really indulging in the fantasy that public schools can do a job that parents and churches are failing to do. Even though American ignorance about religion is clearly a byproduct of more general cultural ignorance, people of faith ought to be discomfited by Americans' shaky grasp of the tenets of even their own religions. There is something truly out of kilter in a society in which Christian fundamentalists take up arms in the culture wars in order to install the Ten Commandments in courthouses and ignore the fact that so many Americans (including politicians who have supported these efforts) do not know exactly what the commandments say.

Perhaps the push for more religious symbols in public life is really a confession of the private failures of families, and the institutional failure of churches, to educate their young in religious traditions.

Three-quarters of Americans even hold the erroneous belief that the Bible says, "God helps those who help themselves."

This non-Biblical saying is certainly made to order for those who don't believe in government aid to the poor; it enables them to worship Christ and the unregulated "free market."

The real problem is that we are an increasingly ignorant people, in thrall to endless infotainment and unwilling to devote time to the serious reading required to transmit any aspect of culture—including religion. How pathetic it is that we are talking about classes to summarize the role of the Bible in culture as a substitute for actually reading the Bible.

As Thomas Jefferson memorably said in 1816, "If a nation expects to be ignorant and free, in a state of civilization, it expects what never was and never will be."

EVALUATING THE AUTHOR'S ARGUMENTS:

In this viewpoint Susan Jacoby argues that religion should not be taught in public schools. Name one point of agreement and one point of disagreement between Jacoby and Michael Tracey, author of the previous viewpoint.

Should Public Schools Teach Alternatives to Evolution?

The teaching of evolution in schools has been a controversial issue since 1925, when a Tennessee law banned the subject from the classroom.

Evolution Should Be Taught in Public Schools Without Alternatives

"Despite the constant claims of creationists to the contrary, there simply is no debate among scientists about the validity of evolution."

Steven Newton

In the following viewpoint Steven Newton argues that there is no debate about the validity of the theory of evolution and that any creationist alternatives to evolution do not belong in science classrooms. Newton claims that creationists have argued that evidence against evolution should be included in science classrooms, when no such evidence exists. He concludes that although there is debate about how evolution occurred, only the teaching of evolution belongs in science classrooms as an explanation for the origin of life. Newton is programs and policy director for the National Center for Science Education, a nonprofit organization defending the teaching of evolution in public schools.

Steven Newton, "Creationists Have Gotten Clever, but There's Still No Debate over Evolution," *Christian Science Monitor,* January 19, 2011. Reproduced by permission of the author.

AS YOU READ, CONSIDER THE FOLLOWING QUESTIONS:
1. According to the author, in what year did a federal court in Pennsylvania conclude that teaching intelligent design in public schools is unconstitutional?
2. What scientific organization does Newton say has publicly stated that there is no controversy about evolution.
3. The author states that what evolutionary biologist has been quoted out of context to imply that the theory of evolution was no longer tenable?

A s 2011 gets under way, those who care about the integrity of science education are bracing for the latest round of state legislation aimed at undermining the teaching of evolution in the public schools. Every year, a host of these bills are filed across the country. In 2008, one was passed in Louisiana, despite protests from scientists and educators. In Oklahoma, State Senator Josh Brecheen (R) has vowed to introduce a bill in the coming legislative session that requires schools to teach "all the facts" on the so-called fallacies of evolution. [Brecheen introduced HB 1551, which did not pass.]

The Tactics of Creationists

The tactics of creationists have evolved since 1925, when Tennessee's Butler Act forbade the teaching of evolution, and high school biology teacher John Scopes was put on trial for doing so. (Creationists believe that God created the physical universe and all organisms according to the account in Genesis, denying the evolution of species.)

But creationists' tactics have also evolved since 2005, when a federal court in Pennsylvania established that teaching intelligent design (ID) in public schools is unconstitutional. The judge in the case ruled, "ID is not science" and derives instead from "religious strategies that evolved from earlier forms of creationism." (Intelligent design holds that "certain features of the universe and of living things are best explained by an intelligent cause, not an undirected process such as natural selection.")

The favored strategy of intelligent design proponents and creationists now is to try to undermine the teaching of evolution by arguing

Barrie Callahan, seated, who challenged the teaching of intelligent design in a Pennsylvania federal court, meets with the press to discuss the court's ruling that teaching the subject in public schools is unconstitutional.

that "evidence against evolution" should be taught, in order to foster a spirit of critical inquiry among students. Arguing that students ought to be exposed to an alleged scientific debate over evolution, intelligent design proponents call for a radical rewriting of textbooks and curricula.

The new strategy is craftier—but just as bogus.

No Debate on Evolution

Despite the constant claims of creationists to the contrary, there simply is no debate among scientists about the validity of evolution. If you search research journals and attend scientific conferences, it becomes readily apparent that while there are controversies over the details of evolution, there is no controversy about the basic fact that living things have descended with modification from a common ancestry. Scientists argue how evolution happened, not whether evolution happened.

This doesn't stop creationists from imagining they can conjure a debate by repeating the claim that there is evidence against evolution. Intelligent design advocates claim they aren't asking public schools to teach creationism, just the "scientific debate over Darwinian evolution." The problem, again, is that there is no debate to teach. The National Academy of Sciences, the nation's most prestigious scientific organization, emphasizes, "There is no scientific controversy about the basic facts of evolution."

If there were credible scientific evidence against evolution, scientists would be the first to discover it, the first to publish it in peer-reviewed journals, and the first to debate its validity and importance. After all, discovering credible scientific evidence against evolution would be a revolutionary accomplishment, worthy of a Nobel Prize. That's why accusations from creationists and intelligent design advocates that scientists are conspiring to suppress evidence against evolution are, to put it mildly, silly.

FAST FACT

In its statement on the teaching of evolution, the National Science Teachers Association argues that "teachers should emphasize evolution" and not be pressured "to promote nonscientific views."

Creationists Are Cutting in Line

Because scientists are not debating evolution, it is wrong to teach students otherwise. In public school science classes and textbooks, the basic methods and results of the mainstream scientific consensus are presented—not untested fringe ideas, not speculations, but information fully supported by evidence. By demanding to cut in line, creationists ask to bypass the normal process of verifying scientific claims. They try to misuse public resources to foist their scientifically unwarranted denial of evolution on a captive student audience, and to force their culture war into America's classrooms.

What creationists regard as "scientific evidence" against evolution is really a collection of debunked claims circulating and persisting like urban legends. For example, from the Scopes era to today, creationists

Scientific Consensus on Evolution Not Shared by Public

Humans and other living things have . . .	Public Percent	Scientists Percent
Evolved over time . . .	61	97
due to the natural processes	32	87
guided by supreme being	22	8
Existed in their present form since the beginning of time	31	2

Taken from: Pew Research Center, "Scientific Achievements Less Prominent than a Decade Ago: Public Praises Science; Scientists Fault Public, Media," July 9, 2009, p. 37.

have eagerly cited the so-called Cambrian explosion, a 10-million-year period about 530 million years ago when fossils record a blossoming of animal life. Creationists claim that the standard model of evolutionary change is incapable of explaining how so many new kinds of animals could have flourished so quickly.

As Mr. Brecheen, the Oklahoma state senator, recently garbled it, "The main fallacy with Darwinian theory is the sudden appearance at about 540 million years [ago] of fossil records." (In fact, the earliest fossils were formed about three billion years earlier than that.) The Cambrian explosion, he wrote, "debunks the tree of life"—a view not shared by practicing paleontologists.

Creationism Is Bad Science

Lacking any substantive evidence to make their case, creationists offer a few selective quotes from real scientists to give their arguments authority. For example, noted National Institutes of Health evolutionary biologist Eugene V. Koonin was recently quoted by a program officer with the leading intelligent design organization (the Discovery Institute) as saying that the modern synthesis of evolution has "crumbled, apparently, beyond repair." The implication was that Mr. Koonin would agree that there is a scientific debate over evolution that deserves to be taught in the schools.

But when I talked to Koonin, he told me this interpretation was simply wrong. Creationists, he said, "delight in claiming that whenever any aspect of '(neo)Darwinism' is considered obsolete, evolution is denied. Nothing could be further from the truth." Koonin explained that what is "crumbling" in his view is a half-century-old approach to thinking about evolution. Modern evolutionary theory is "a much broader, richer and ultimately more satisfactory constellation of data, concepts, and ideas." Evolution is alive and well, while creationist understanding of it is apparently stuck in the [President Dwight D.] Eisenhower era.

Whether by banning the teaching of evolution, or requiring the teaching of creation science or intelligent design, or encouraging the teaching of long-ago-debunked misrepresentations of evolution, creationist proposals are bad science, bad pedagogy, and bad policy. Instead of proposing scientifically illiterate and educationally harmful measures, state legislatures—and other policy-makers—should help students learn about evolution. As the geneticist Theodosius Dobzhansky famously said—and as Eugene Koonin explicitly agreed—"Nothing in biology makes sense except in the light of evolution."

EVALUATING THE AUTHOR'S ARGUMENTS:

In this viewpoint Steven Newton argues that there is no debate about evolution among scientists. How does David Fowler, author of the following viewpoint, attempt to undermine this claim?

Criticism of Evolution Should Be Taught in Public Schools

David Fowler

"We need more science teaching, not less."

In the following viewpoint David Fowler argues that it is a mistake to limit discussion of the origin of species to Darwinian evolution without discussing weaknesses and criticism of evolution. Fowler contends that the scientific community has been trying to use the law to keep criticism of Darwinian evolution out of the public school science classroom. Consequently, he argues that there is a need for a law that specifically permits science teachers to discuss weaknesses in Darwinian evolution. Fowler is the president of the Family Action Council of Tennessee.

AS YOU READ, CONSIDER THE FOLLOWING QUESTIONS:

1. What law does Fowler say has been used to prevent teaching evolution in Tennessee's public school science classes?
2. To what statement do 850 doctorate-level scientists subscribe, according to the author?
3. According to Fowler, what does Tennessee Senate Bill 893/ House Bill 368 permit?

David Fowler, "Making Scopes Proud—Finally—and Response," www.Chattanoogan.com, February 21, 2011. Reproduced by permission of the author.

John Scopes, the Rhea County schoolteacher who in 1925 stood trial for violating a Tennessee law prohibiting the teaching of evolution, would surely support new legislation pending before the General Assembly. After 86 years, Tennessee lawmakers have a chance to get the "scope" of science instruction right.

The crux of the infamous Scopes trial was the Tennessee General Assembly's effort to reduce, by law, the scope of what could be taught in the science classroom, namely, to prevent the then relatively new

John Scopes, a Rhea County, Tennessee, schoolteacher, stood trial in 1925 for teaching evolution in his classroom.

theory of Darwinian evolution from being taught in the science class-
room. The law was called the Butler Act, named after state Rep.
John Butler, head of an organization known as the World's Christian
Fundamentals Association.

But now the shoe is on the other foot, and the scientific community, generally speaking, wants to use the law to limit the scope of what
can be taught in science class,
and they often seek to impugn
any school of thought critical of
Darwinian evolution.

FAST FACT

Tennessee's Butler Act,
which prohibited public
school teachers from teaching evolution, was not
repealed until 1967.

For example, one high school
science teacher in Tennessee last
year did her best to make sure
that students didn't get a balanced understanding of intelligent design. The theory of intelligent design holds that certain
features of the universe and of
living things are best explained by an intelligent cause, not an undirected process such as natural selection.

Now Tennessee does not require the teaching of intelligent design.
In fact, the curriculum standard for Tennessee on the subject of evolution is one of the most one-sided, pro-evolution standards in the
country. It provides that students shall be able to "summarize the
supporting evidence for the theory of evolution." No mention is given
to the educational value of learning how to think critically about the
state of the scientific evidence on evolution and to know both the
strengths and weaknesses of that evidence.

But this teacher apparently wanted to make sure she didn't do
anything to undermine her students' understanding of the evidence
"supporting" evolution. She brought up intelligent design, a rival
theory to evolution, and then made sure it was discredited. In fact,
after having her class watch a rather one-sided PBS documentary
decrying the theory of intelligent design, she then had her students
write an essay about what they learned. To assist with the paper she
provided students with writing prompts such as:

Why is evolution the only current acceptable scientific theory to
explain the origin of the species?

How is bias a problem with [Intelligent Design] Theory?

What religion is spearheading the intelligent design movement?

And the coup de grace for the lesson on intelligent design was the prompt for the final paragraph:

Why is the separation of church and state so vital to the foundation and continuation of our way of life in America?

Certainly intelligent design theory is not without its critics, and if the subject is going to be taught, then discussion of those criticisms is appropriate. But it is also appropriate that students understand that intelligent design is a theory that many scientists are beginning to consider and hold because of the weaknesses in the scientific evidence supporting evolution. In fact, over 850 PhD-level scientists from some of the finest universities around the world have subscribed to this statement:

We are skeptical of claims for the ability of random mutation and natural selection to account for the complexity of life. Careful examination of the evidence for Darwinian theory should be encouraged.

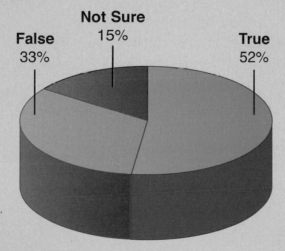

Americans' Beliefs and Knowledge About Human Evolution

The theory of evolution proposes missing links and speculates about how humans developed but does not have strong factual evidence to support it.

Not Sure 15%

False 33%

True 52%

Taken from: Harris Interactive survey, Americans' Beliefs and Knowledge About Creationism, the Role of God, "Intelligent Design," and Human Evolution, July–October 2009.

The point is this: We need more science teaching, not less. In fact, today's evolutionary scientists have become the modern-day equivalents of the legislators who passed the Butler Act. They want to limit even an objective discussion of the scientific strengths and weaknesses of evolutionary theory.

To correct this problem, state Rep. Bill Dunn and state Sen. Bo Watson have filed legislation (Senate Bill 893/House Bill 368) that would permit science teachers "to help students understand, analyze, critique, and review in an objective manner the scientific strengths and scientific weaknesses of existing scientific theories covered in the course being taught." Note that the law does not require the teaching of intelligent design or creationism since they are not '"scientific theories" that are being "covered in the course[s] being taught" in Tennessee. And the law is clear that the teacher is limited to discussing scientific evidence.

But the bill does one more important thing. The bill would make clear that no teacher can be disciplined for helping students evaluate all the evidence on the subject. Such a law in 1925 would have protected John Scopes.

Thus my bet is John Scopes might say that, with this bill, the Tennessee legislature has a chance to finally get it right when it comes to teaching science on the subject of evolution. They get their first chance this Wednesday when the bill comes up for its first hearing in the House Subcommittee on Education.

EVALUATING THE AUTHOR'S ARGUMENTS:

In this viewpoint David Fowler argues that criticism of Darwinian evolution should be taught in public school science classrooms. Name one other author from this chapter who agrees with Fowler and one who disagrees with him. Explain your answers.

"*Teach science in the public schools, but don't conveniently leave out valid scientific evidence or theories that might contradict evolution.*"

Scientific Creationism Should Be Taught in Public Schools

Henry Morris III

In the following viewpoint Henry Morris III argues that the study of scientific evidence in support of creationism should be allowed into public school classrooms. He claims that despite widespread belief in creationism, teaching the subject is not allowed in public schools. Morris says that disallowing the teaching of creationism follows a pattern of viewpoint discrimination that exists at all levels of education. He claims that students should be allowed to be exposed to the all competing scientific theories to evolution, including scientific creationism. Morris is executive vice president for strategic ministries of the Institute for Creation Research in Dallas, Texas.

Henry Morris III, "Where Evolution Has Gaps, Creation Might Offer Answers—If We Will Listen," *US News & World Report*, February 2, 2009. Reprinted with permission.

AS YOU READ, CONSIDER THE FOLLOWING QUESTIONS:
  1. Morris identifies what two problems with the theory of evolution?
  2. What three forms of creationism does the author identify?
  3. What example does Morris give to support his claim that private schools have been persecuted for teaching creationism?

Duncing this last campaign [2008], the topic of science—specifically, creationism and evolution—was pushed out onto the stage of the presidential debates. So much so that *USA Today*/Gallup released the results of a poll in which 66 percent of Americans stated that they believe in creationism. Not some hybrid theory mixing creationism and evolution. Not intelligent design. But specifically that "God created human beings pretty much in their present form at one time within the last 10,000 years." Which is pretty much how the book of Genesis explains creation.

Last year, the *St. Petersburg* (Fla.) *Times* conducted its own poll on teaching creationism in the public schools. Not surprisingly, nearly two thirds of registered voters were not convinced of evolution's merits.

Creationism in Public School

However, despite public opinion on the issue, creationism, in any form, is not allowed in our classrooms.

Should it be? Americans seem to prefer it, or at a minimum favor a critical discussion of the strengths and weaknesses of evolution. Even the National Science Teachers Association—hardly a right-wing fundamentalist group—insists that "teachers must be free to examine controversial issues openly in the classroom . . . to maintain a spirit of free inquiry, open-mindedness and impartiality in the classroom."

So, what kind of science is being taught to our children today? A *philosophy* of science, actually, rooted in a worldview that deliberately disbelieves in anything supernatural. No God. No angels. No Intelligent Designer. Everything happened quite by accident.

The idea of origins by accident (evolution), which Charles Darwin popularized 150 years ago, is now characterized as a bona fide scientific theory. Embarrassingly, this "theory" cannot be scientifically observed in action today, nor can it be forensically observed in nature's record of the past. But it is, nonetheless, believed. And so ardent are its followers that many scientists refuse to admit the weaknesses of this doctrine, let alone "allow a divine foot in the door," as Harvard's Richard Lewontin warns.

In Texas, state school board officials are debating the language of science education standards for our public schools and whether teachers should even be allowed to discuss evolution's weaknesses. The idea of teaching creation science in the classroom isn't even under consideration.

Opponents of Creationism
And yet, the opponents of creationism would have the public believe that Bible-believing teachers constitute some sort of threat to education.

For instance, when scientists from the Seattle-based Discovery Institute arrived on the campus of Southern Methodist University [SMU] in 2007 to present evidence for intelligent design, the SMU

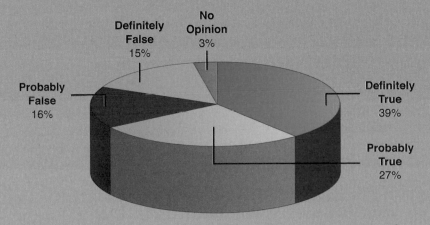

Americans' Views on Creationism

What is your view on creationism, that is, the idea that God created human beings pretty much in their present form at one time within the last 10,000 years?

Definitely False 15%

No Opinion 3%

Probably False 16%

Definitely True 39%

Probably True 27%

Taken from: Gallup Poll, "Evolution, Creationism, Intelligent Design," June 1–3, 2007. www.gallup.com/poll/21814/Evolution-Creationism-Intelligent-Design.aspx.

science faculty refused to sit down, even behind closed doors, and discuss, peer-to-peer, the scientific data. Perhaps they were afraid a "divine foot" would somehow gain a toehold in this bastion of Methodist education.

Oxford evolutionary biologist Richard Dawkins spends more time lecturing about God (and Dawkins's disbelief in him) than he does actually doing science. Dawkins's strange admission in the *Expelled* documentary that highly intelligent aliens may have seeded life on

British evolutionary biologist Richard Dawkins has come under fire from intelligent design theorists for not providing credible scientific proof of evolution.

Earth only compounds the problem that evolutionists continue to have in demonstrating reasonable scientific data for their monkey-to-man theory.

The Need for Scientific Creationism

The question of whether creationism should be part of the educational experience in American schools can best be answered by the father of the modern creation science movement, the late Henry Morris.

Morris detailed three basic forms of creationism: scientific creationism—the study of scientific evidence alone; biblical creationism—the study of the Bible alone; and scientific-biblical creationism—the study of both science and the Bible.

FAST FACT

In a 2009 poll, a plurality of Americans agreed with this statement: "All of the events recorded in the Old Testament of the Bible are supported by archaeological evidence."

Which should be taught in public schools? Quite clearly, Morris stated that "creationists should not advocate that biblical creationism be taught in public schools, both because of judicial restrictions against religion in such schools and also (more importantly) because teachers who do not *believe* the Bible should not be asked to *teach* the Bible."

Teach science in the public schools, but don't conveniently leave out valid scientific evidence or theories that might contradict evolution. But are students genuinely allowed a "spirit of free inquiry" in the classroom? Like in higher education? Think again.

Discrimination Against Opposing Viewpoints

Ben Stein's *Expelled* documentary revealed that highly qualified scientists in academia have become victims of viewpoint discrimination for openly acknowledging evidence for design that contradicts evolution.

The more alarming problem that has arisen in this controversy, however, is the persecution of private schools that choose to teach any form of origins science other than evolution. One case in point is the University of California's refusal to nondiscriminatorily admit students from private Christian schools that included openly creation-ist viewpoints in their courses.

Another case is our own Institute for Creation Research Graduate School, which has offered master's degrees in the sciences for 27 years. State officials refused to approve the move of the school's program to Texas because of its institutional viewpoint. Ironically, this is the same Texas agency the Texas Supreme Court ruled against for unconstitutionally violating the First Amendment rights of three other private schools in 2007. Remember, these are private schools that merely wanted to teach curricula reflecting their institutional beliefs. Where's the ACLU [American Civil Liberties Union] when you need it?

While state legislatures haggle over the words science, theory, and weaknesses, American schoolchildren continue to rank poorly in science education among the nations of the world. Pouring more money into the status quo of evolution-based science education isn't the answer. Teaching the truth is.

EVALUATING THE AUTHOR'S ARGUMENTS:

In this viewpoint Henry Morris III contends that scientific creationism should be taught even though it contradicts evolution. Why do the National Academy of Sciences and the Institute of Medicine of the National Academies, authors of the following viewpoint, disagree? With which viewpoint do you agree? Explain your reasoning.

Creationism Should Not Be Taught in Public Schools

National Academy of Sciences and Institute of Medicine of the National Academies

"Teaching creationist ideas in science classes confuses what constitutes science and what does not."

In the following viewpoint the National Academy of Sciences (NAS) and the Institute of Medicine of the National Academies (IOM) argue that creationism does not belong in science classrooms. The NAS and the IOM contend that there is no scientific evidence for creationism. Furthermore, the authors deny the creationist claim that because evolution has not been directly observed, it is not scientifically supported. The NAS and the IOM conclude that nonscientific material, such as the theory of creationism, is not science and should not be taught as such. The NAS is an honorific society of distinguished scholars engaged in scientific research for use for the general welfare. The IOM is an independent, nonprofit organization that works outside of government to provide unbiased advice to the public.

"Creationist Perspectives," *Science, Evolution, and Creationism.* Washington, DC: National Academies Press, 2008. © 2008 by the National Academy of Sciences. Reproduced by permission.

AS YOU READ, CONSIDER THE FOLLOWING QUESTIONS:
1. The authors contend that scientific evidence indicate the earth is how old?
2. The National Academy of Sciences and Institute of Medicine of the National Academies claim that dinosaurs became extinct approximately how long before humans evolved?
3. Why do the authors say that all students need a good education in science?

Advocates of the ideas collectively known as "creationism" and, recently, "intelligent design creationism" hold a wide variety of views. Most broadly, a "creationist" is someone who rejects natural scientific explanations of the known universe in favor of special creation by a supernatural entity. Creationism in its various forms is not the same thing as belief in God because . . . many believers as well as many mainstream religious groups accept the findings of science, including evolution. Nor is creationism necessarily tied to Christians who interpret the Bible literally. Some non-Christian religious believers also want to replace scientific explanations with their own religion's supernatural accounts of physical phenomena.

The Views of Creationism

In the United States, various views of creationism typically have been promoted by small groups of politically active religious fundamentalists who believe that only a supernatural entity could account for the physical changes in the universe and for the biological diversity of life on Earth. But even these creationists hold very different views. Some, known as "young Earth" creationists, believe the biblical account that the universe and the Earth were created just a few thousand years ago. Proponents of this form of creationism also believe that all living things, including humans, were created in a very short period of time in essentially the forms in which they exist today. Other creationists, known as "old Earth" creationists, accept that the Earth may be very old but reject other scientific findings regarding the evolution of living things.

No scientific evidence supports these viewpoints. On the contrary . . . several independent lines of evidence indicate that the Earth is about 4.5 billion years old and that the universe is about 14 billion years old. Rejecting the evidence for these age estimates would mean rejecting not just biological evolution but also fundamental discoveries of modern physics, chemistry, astrophysics, and geology.

Some creationists believe that Earth's present form and the distribution of fossils can be explained by a worldwide flood. But this claim also is at odds with observations and evidence understood scientifically. The belief that Earth's sediments, with their fossils, were deposited in a short period does not accord either with the known processes of sedimentation or with the estimated volume of water needed to deposit sediments on the top of some of Earth's highest mountains.

The Fossil Record

Creationists sometimes cite what they claim to be an incomplete fossil record as evidence that living things were created in their modern forms. But this argument ignores the rich and extremely detailed record of evolutionary history that paleontologists and other biologists have constructed over the past two centuries and are continuing to construct. Paleontological research has filled in many of the parts of the fossil record that were incomplete in Charles Darwin's time. The claim that the fossil record is "full of gaps" that undermine evolution is simply false. Indeed, paleontologists now know enough about the ages of sediments to predict where they will be able to find particularly significant transitional fossils, as happened with *Tiktaalik* and the ancestors of modern humans. Researchers also are using new techniques, such as computed axial tomography (CT), to learn even more about the internal structures and composition of delicate bones of fossils. Exciting new discoveries of fossils continue to be reported in both the scientific literature and popular media.

Another compelling feature of the fossil record is its consistency. Nowhere on Earth are fossils from dinosaurs, which went extinct

FAST FACT

According to a 2009 poll, only 17 percent of Americans said that creationism, which says that human beings were created directly by God, should be taught in schools.

"INTELLIGENT DESIGN"
(the one by our founding fathers)

CHURCH

Religion goes here

STATE

Science goes here

Public Schools

A LARGE HIGH WALL

M. WUERKER

© 2005 Matt Wuerker. Used with the permission of Matt Wuerker and the Cartoonist Group. All rights reserved.

65 million years ago, found together with fossils from humans, who evolved in just the last few million years. Nowhere are the fossils of mammals found in sediments that are more than about 220 million years old. Whenever creationists point to sediments where these relationships appear to be altered or even reversed, scientists have clearly

demonstrated that this reversal has resulted from the folding of geological strata over or under others. Sediments containing the fossils of only unicellular organisms appear earlier in the fossil record than do sediments containing the remains of both unicellular and multicellular organisms. The sequence of fossils across Earth's sediments points unambiguously toward the occurrence of evolution.

The Role of Observation in Science

Creationists sometimes argue that the idea of evolution must remain hypothetical because "no one has ever seen evolution occur." This kind of statement also reveals that some creationists misunderstand an important characteristic of scientific reasoning. Scientific conclusions are not limited to direct observation but often depend on inferences that are made by applying reason to observations. Even with the launch of Earth-orbiting spacecraft, scientists could not directly see the Earth going around the Sun. But they inferred from a wealth of independent measurements that the Sun is at the center of the solar system. Until the recent development of extremely powerful microscopes, scientists could not observe atoms, but the behavior of physical objects left no doubt about the atomic nature of matter. Scientists hypothesized the existence of viruses for many years before microscopes became powerful enough to see them.

Thus, for many areas of science, scientists have not directly observed the objects (such as genes and atoms) or the phenomena (such as the Earth going around the Sun) that are now well-established facts. Instead, they have confirmed them indirectly by observational and experimental evidence. Evolution is no different. Indeed . . . evolutionary science provides one of the best examples of a deep understanding based on scientific reasoning.

This contention that nobody has seen evolution occurring further ignores the overwhelming evidence that evolution has taken place and is continuing to occur. The annual changes in influenza viruses and the emergence of bacteria resistant to antibiotics are both products of evolutionary forces. Another example of ongoing evolution is the appearance of mosquitoes resistant to various insecticides, which has contributed to a resurgence of malaria in Africa and elsewhere. The transitional fossils that have been found in abundance since Darwin's time reveal how species continually give rise to successor species that, over time, produce radically changed body forms and functions. It also is possible to directly observe many of the specific processes by which evolution occurs. Scientists regularly do experiments using microbes and other model systems that directly test evolutionary hypotheses.

Creationists reject such scientific facts in part because they do not accept evidence drawn from natural processes that they consider to be at odds with the Bible. But science cannot test supernatural possibilities. To young Earth creationists, no amount of empirical evidence that the Earth is billions of years old is likely to refute their claim that the world is actually young but that God simply made it *appear* to be old. Because such appeals to the supernatural are not testable using the rules and processes of scientific inquiry, they cannot be a part of science. . . .

Creationism Is Unscientific

The arguments of creationists reverse the scientific process. They begin with an explanation that they are unwilling to alter—that supernatural forces have shaped biological or Earth systems—rejecting the basic requirements of science that hypotheses must be restricted to testable natural explanations. Their beliefs cannot be tested, modified, or rejected by scientific means and thus cannot be a part of the processes of science.

Despite the lack of scientific evidence for creationist positions, some advocates continue to demand that various forms of creationism be taught together with or in place of evolution in science classes. Many teachers are under considerable pressure from policy makers, school administrators, parents, and students to downplay or eliminate the teaching of evolution. As a result, many U.S. students lack access to information and ideas that are both integral to modern science and essential for making informed, evidence-based decisions about their own lives and our collective future.

Regardless of the careers that they ultimately select, to succeed in today's scientifically and technologically sophisticated world, *all* students need a sound education in science. Many of today's fast-growing and high-paying jobs require a familiarity with the core concepts, applications, and implications of science. To make informed decisions about public policies, people need to know how scientific evidence supports those policies and whether that evidence was gathered using well-established scientific practice and principles. Learning about evolution is an excellent way to help students understand the nature, processes, and limits of science in addition to concepts about this fundamentally important contribution to scientific knowledge.

Given the importance of science in all aspects of modern life, the science curriculum should not be undermined with nonscientific material. Teaching creationist ideas in science classes confuses what constitutes science and what does not. It compromises the objectives of public education and the goal of a high-quality science education.

EVALUATING THE AUTHOR'S ARGUMENTS:

In this viewpoint the National Academy of Sciences and the Institute of Medicine of the National Academies deny that creationism is science. What would they say about the possibility of teaching scientific creationism, as proposed by Henry Morris III in the previous viewpoint?

PCHS Media Center
Grant, Nebraska

Intelligent Design Should Be Allowed to Be Taught in Public Schools

"One can teach about creationism without advocating it, just as one can teach in a history lesson about totalitarianism without advocating it."

Michael Reiss

In the following viewpoint Michael Reiss argues that intelligent design, a theory that agrees with creationism but makes no reference to the Scriptures, should be taught in public schools. Reiss claims that intelligent design is a worldview that has its place in science classrooms, just as evolution does. The theory of evolution is no more than a theory itself, Reiss argues. Intelligent design and evolution do not have to be compatible in order to be taught side-by-side, he concludes.

Michael Reiss is a professor of science education at the Institute of England, University of London. He holds a doctorate in evolutionary biology, and he is a priest in the Church of England.

Michael Reiss, "Should Creationism Be Taught in British Classrooms?," *New Statesman,* April 6, 2010. Copyright © 2010 New Statesman, Ltd. Reproduced by permission.

AS YOU READ, CONSIDER THE FOLLOWING QUESTIONS:
1. What does the author list as the primary argument for intelligent design?
2. What did philosopher of science Phillip Kitcher conclude about creationism in a study published in 1983?
3. How does Reiss respond to the claim of scientists who believe that consideration of intelligent design and creationism in a classroom setting legitimizes the theories?

To some people's incredulity and others' satisfaction, creationism's influence is growing across the globe. Definitions of creationism vary, but roughly 10–15 per cent of people in the UK believe that the earth came into existence exactly as described in the early parts of the Bible or the Quran, and that the most that evolution has done is to change species into other, closely related species.

The more recent theory of intelligent design agrees with creationism, but makes no reference to the scriptures. Instead, it argues that there are many features of the natural world—such as the mammalian eye—that are too intricate to have evolved from non-living matter, as the theory of evolution asserts. Such features are simply said to be "irreducibly complex".

At the same time, the overwhelming majority of biologists consider evolution to be central to the biological sciences, providing a conceptual framework that unifies every disparate aspect of the life sciences into a single, coherent discipline. Most scientists also believe that the universe is about 13–14 billion years old.

The well-known schism between a number of religious world-views—particularly Christian views based on Genesis and mainstream Islamic readings of the Quran—and scientific explanations derived from the theory of evolution is exacerbated by the way people are asked in surveys about their views on the origins of human life.

The Relationship Between Religion and Science

There is a tendency to polarise religion and science: questions focus on the notion that either God created everything, or God had nothing to do with it. The choices erroneously imply that scientific evolution is necessarily atheistic, linking acceptance of evolution with the explicit exclusion of any religious premise.

In fact, people have personal beliefs about religion and science that cover a wide range of possibilities. This has important implications for how biology teachers should present evolution in schools. As John Hedley Brooke, the first holder of the Andreas Idreos Professorship of Science and Religion at Oxford University, has long pointed out, there is no such thing as a fixed relationship between science and religion. The interface between them has shifted over time, as has the meaning of each term.

Most of the literature on creationism (and intelligent design) and evolutionary theory puts them in stark opposition. Evolution is consistently presented in creationist books and articles as illogical, contradicted by scientific evidence such as the fossil record (which they claim does not provide evidence for transitional forms), and as the product of non-scientific reasoning. The early history of life, they say, would require life to arise from inorganic matter—a form of spontaneous generation largely rejected by science in the 19th century. Creationists also accuse evolutionary theory of being the product of those who ridicule the word of God, and a cause of a range of social evils (from eugenics, Marxism, Nazism and racism to juvenile delinquency).

Creationism has received similarly short shrift from evolutionists. In a study published in 1983, the philosopher of science Philip Kitcher concluded that the flat-earth theory, the chemistry of the four elements and medieval astrology were all as valid as creationism (not at all, that is).

Life Lessons

Evolutionary biologists attack creationism—especially "scientific creationism"—on the grounds that it isn't a science at all, because its ultimate authority is scriptural and theological, rather than the evidence obtained from the natural world.

After many years of teaching evolution to school and university students, I have come to the view that creationism is best seen by science teachers not as a misconception, but as a world-view. A world-

Intelligent design proponent Michael Behe, pictured, and his colleague William Dembski say they have developed criteria for testing intelligent design theory.

view is an entire way of understanding reality: each of us probably has only one.

However, we can have many conceptions and misconceptions. The implications of this for education is that the most a science teacher can normally hope to achieve is to ensure that students with creationist beliefs understand the basic scientific position. Over the course of a few school lessons or a run of university lectures, it is unlikely that a teacher will be able to replace a creationist world-view with a scientific one.

So how might one teach evolution in science lessons to 14- to 16-year-olds? The first thing to note is that there is scope for young people to discuss beliefs about human origins in other subjects, notably religious education. In England, the DCSF (Department for Children, Schools and Families) and the QCA (Qualifications and Curriculum Authority) have published a non-statutory national framework for religious education and a teaching unit that asks: "How can we answer questions about creation and origins?" The unit focuses on creation and the origins of the universe and human life, as well as the relationships between religion and science. As you might expect, the unit is open-ended and is all about getting young people to learn about different views and develop their own thinking. But what should we do in science?

FAST FACT

According to a 2008 survey, 47 percent of high school biology teachers believe that humans developed over time with God guiding the process, and 16 percent believe God created humans in their present form in the last 10,000 years.

In summer 2007, after months of behind-the-scenes meetings, the DCSF guidance on creationism and intelligent design received ministerial approval and was published. As one of those who helped put the guidance together, I was relieved when it was welcomed. Even the discussions on the RichardDawkins.net forum were positive, while the *Freethinker*, an atheist journal, described it as "a breath of fresh air" and "a model of clarity and reason".

Theories Are Just Ideas

The guidance points out that the use of the word "theory" in science (as in "the theory of evolution") can be misleading, as it is different from the everyday meaning—that is, of being little more than an idea. In science, the word indicates that there is substantial supporting evidence, underpinned by principles and explanations accepted by the international scientific community. The guidance makes clear that creationism and intelligent design do not constitute scientific theories.

Theories Studied in High School Biology Classes, 2007

Hours Taught	Human Evolution	General Evolutionary Processes	Creationism or Intelligent Design
Not covered	17%	2%	75%
1–2 hours	35%	9%	18%
3–5 hours	25%	25%	5%
6–10 hours	12%	26%	1%
11–15 hours	5%	18%	1%
16–20 hours	3%	11%	1%
20 hours or more	2%	9%	0%
Total*	100%	100%	100%

*Figures are approximate, due to rounding.

Taken from: Michael B. Berkman, Julianna Sandell Pacheco, and Eric Plutzer, "Evolution and Creationism in America's Classrooms: A National Portrait," *PLoS Biology*, May 20, 2008.

It also illuminates that there is a real difference between teaching something and teaching about something. In other words, one can teach about creationism without advocating it, just as one can teach in a history lesson about totalitarianism without advocating it.

This is a key point. Many scientists, and some science teachers, fear that consideration of creationism or intelligent design in a science classroom legitimises them. That something lacks scientific support, however, doesn't seem to me a sufficient reason to omit it from a science lesson.

I remember being excited, when I was taught physics at school, that we could discuss almost anything, provided we were prepared to defend our thinking in a way that admitted objective evidence and logical argument. I recall one of our A-level chemistry teachers scoffing at a fellow student, who reported that she had sat (outside the lesson) with a spoon in front of her while [psychic] Uri Geller maintained he could bend viewers' spoons [with his mind]. I was all for her approach. After all, I reasoned, surely the first thing was to establish if the spoon bent (it didn't for her), and if it did, to start working out how.

Free Expression

When teaching evolution, there is much to be said for allowing students to raise any doubts they have in order to shape and provoke a genuine discussion. The word "genuine" doesn't mean that creationism and intelligent design deserve equal time with evolution. They don't. However, in certain classes, depending on the teacher's comfort with talking about such issues, his or her ability to deal with them, and the make-up of the student body, it can and should be appropriate to address them.

Having said that, I don't pretend to think that this kind of teaching is easy. Some students become very heated; others remain silent even if they disagree profoundly with what is said. But I believe in taking seriously the concerns of students who do not accept the theory of evolution while still introducing them to it. Although it is unlikely that this will help them resolve any conflict they experience between science and their beliefs, good teaching can help students to manage it—and to learn more science.

My hope is simply to enable students to understand the scientific perspective with respect to our origins, but not necessarily to accept it. We can help students to find their science lessons interesting and intellectually challenging without their being a threat. Effective teaching in this area can help students not only learn about the theory of evolution, but also better appreciate the way science is done, the procedures by which scientific knowledge accumulates, the limitations of science and the ways in which scientific knowledge differs from other forms of knowledge.

> ## EVALUATING THE AUTHOR'S ARGUMENTS:
>
> In this viewpoint Michael Reiss argues that the theory of intelligent design should be taught in schools. What is the main point of disagreement between Reiss and Todd Huffman, author of the following viewpoint? With which author do you agree? Explain your answer.

Intelligent Design Does Not Belong in Science Classrooms

Todd Huffman

"Science and faith cannot be taught alongside each other. They are different modes of knowing, different sources of wisdom."

In the following viewpoint Todd Huffman argues that the theory of intelligent design (ID) is not a scientific rival to evolution. Huffman claims that there are no facts that could prove or disprove the theory of ID and, hence, belief in it is a matter of faith. In contrast, Huffman contends that evolution is an evidence-based assumption with testable predictions—a scientific theory. Huffman does not deny that ID is a theory worth discussing, but he claims that to do so in the science classroom alongside evolution is to make the mistake of seeing faith and science as being in competition with each other.

Huffman is a pediatrician and writer in Eugene, Oregon.

Todd Huffman, "Intelligent Design Not Testable; It Can't Be a Scientific Theory," *Register-Guard* (Eugene, OR), July 9, 2006, p. F1. Reproduced by permission of the author.

AS YOU READ, CONSIDER THE FOLLOWING QUESTIONS:
  1. What 1987 US Supreme Court decision found the teaching of creationism in public schools to be unconstitutional, according to Huffman?
  2. According to the author, the theory of evolution by natural selection is the logical conclusion of how many years of experiments, observations, and discoveries?
  3. What does Huffman say about the ability of science to prove or disprove the theory of intelligent design?

In late December [2005], U.S. District Court Judge John Jones III handed down his decision in a lawsuit filed by 11 parents against the school board of Dover, a sleepy Pennsylvania town near the capital, Harrisburg.

In terms of impact, his sweeping judgment was perhaps the most important in American jurisprudence regarding the education of children as to the origins of life since the 1925 Scopes Monkey Trial.

Intelligent Design in the Court

In 2004, an eight-member majority of the Dover School Board mandated a brief disclaimer before pupils were taught about evolution. It stated: "Because Darwin's theory is a theory, it is still being tested as new evidence is being discovered. The theory is not a fact. Gaps in the theory exist for which there is no evidence."

Curious students were encouraged to check out from the school library a specific textbook placed by the school board that offered a theologically-based alternative to Darwin's theory.

While these actions at first may seem innocuous, understand that these eight school board members—every one of them voted out of office last November [2009]—were very public advocates of the idea of "intelligent design," also known as ID, a faith-based alternative to Darwin's theory of evolution. The suit brought by the Dover parents therefore charged the school board with mandating the promotion and dissemination of a religious doctrine in public schools, in violation of the establishment clause of the First Amendment. In a lengthy and broadly written verdict, Judge Jones agreed, ruling that the school board was guilty of "breathtaking inanity." But few believe his decision marks the end of the saga.

Intelligent design emerged after the 1987 Supreme Court decision in *Edwards vs. Aguillard* declared the teaching of creationism in public schools unconstitutional, and was championed by the Discovery Institute, a Seattle-based think tank. It presents itself as an alternative scientific explanation for the evolution of life on Earth. Invoking a complex designer to explain biological diversity, advocates of ID posit that life in all its complexity could not have arisen without the help of an intelligent and guiding hand.

Intelligent Design and Creationism
Intelligent design therefore implies that "God did it," though advocates are careful not to mention the Bible or the divine [by] name. Intelligent designers are even quick to point out that ID is not the modern stepchild of creationism, as is often claimed by its detractors. Creationism applies to the view that life began on Earth approximately 6,000 years ago, and differs from ID in its belief that all living

When the Dover, Pennsylvania, school board, pictured on a campaign billboard, attempted to introduce the teaching of intelligent design in the local school system in 2004, all were voted out of office.

things were divinely created over six literal days and have existed in their present form since the beginning of time.

Supporters of ID accept that the Earth is billions of years old. They do not dispute even whether evolution occurred, but rather how it occurred. Their argument lies in the faith-based belief that an entirely undirected process of natural selection simply cannot account for the extraordinary complexity and diversity of life on this planet.

As a purely theological idea, ID is perfectly understandable. As human beings, we are constantly groping for understanding of this strange and amazing universe into which we are born. How wondrous to think of the universe and nature as divinely inspired, guided and updated.

Nevertheless, while the belief that natural selection is shaped by the active management of an intelligent and heavenly hand is a perfectly legitimate statement of faith, it is only an idea. ID is not a scientific theory, for there is no set of facts that would prove or disprove it. It cannot even be called a hypothesis, for it cannot be tested.

It is therefore intellectually dishonest to present ID as a scientific theory, a valid rival of Darwinian evolution. It is and can only remain exclusively a matter of faith.

FAST FACT

The US District Court for the Middle District of Pennsylvania ruled in *Kitzmiller v. Dover Area School District* (2005) that teaching intelligent design violates the Establishment Clause of the First Amendment.

The Controversy of Evolution

Intelligent designers such as those Dover School Board members say they simply want public schools to give students a more balanced view of evolution. Even President [George W.] Bush agrees. In August 2005, the president endorsed teaching intelligent design alongside evolution: "Both sides ought to be properly taught, so people can understand what the debate is about."

Intelligent designers have seized upon Justice Antonin Scalia's dissent in the 1987 Supreme Court case: "Christian fundamentalists are quite entitled, as a secular matter, to have whatever scientific evidence there may be against evolution presented in their schools." That implication, that "gaps" exist in our modern scientific understanding of evolution and such gaps are easily plugged by God's fingers, lies at the heart of the ID movement, which has as its motto: "Teach the controversy."

However, the controversy to which the president and the ID movement refer lies not within the scientific world, but rather almost entirely within the shape-shifting world of American culture. And to the detriment of more pressing national issues too numerous to count, it is here where the debate over the origins of life will have to be settled.

Through the tactic of demanding that public high school students be taught "the scientific strengths and weaknesses of evolutionary theory," supporters of ID foster what is in fact an illusion—that evolution is a controversial theory among scientists. It is not. Evolution is widely regarded as one of the most powerful and best-supported theories in all of science. It is, as declared recently by the National Academy of Sciences, "the central unifying concept of biology."

It spoke volumes against the idea of intelligent design that after the president's comments last August, the White House felt it necessary to issue a clarification. Presidential science adviser John Marburg told the *New York Times* that ID "is not a scientific concept," and that "evolution is the cornerstone of modern biology." While clashing with the religious beliefs held by many, though by no means all Christians, evolution is an elegant theory that has stood the test of time.

Scientific Theories

Evolution postulates that complex life arises from simple life. Despite more than a century of looking, no one has found any geological evidence proving otherwise, no evidence that the further one went back in time, the more complex life was, or that unrelated species appeared as if from nowhere. Science accepts evolution by natural selection as the logical conclusion of 150 years of countless experiments, observations and geological discoveries.

Evolution is evident not only in the fossil record but also in the letters of the genetic code shared in varying degrees by all species. In

Religious Beliefs Among Scientists

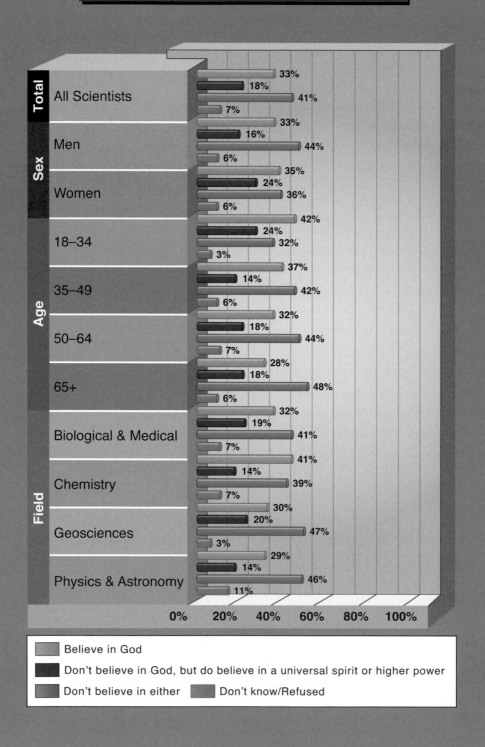

Taken from: Pewforum.org, "Religious Beliefs Among Scientists," May/June 2009.
http://pewforum.org/uploadedimages/Topics/Issues/Science_and_Bioethics/Scientists%20and%20Belief%203.gif.

my field of medicine, evolution is at work every day, when bacteria become more resistant to antibiotics, when cancer cells develop immunity to chemotherapeutic agents and when viruses mutate to become stronger or more contagious. Look no further than HIV, the tuberculosis bacterium or the avian influenza virus for examples of evolution at work.

Much confusion among the public lies with the use of the word "theory." Critics of evolution constantly repeat that evolution is "a theory, not a fact." True, but misleading.

While in common, everyday language "theory" is often synonymous with "hunch" or "educated guess," in science we say "theory" to mean a strong, evidenced-based explanation that brings together many facts and observations in order to make testable predictions.

This is not to say that scientific theories are unassailable. They are not. But to qualify as theories, they must be testable by further research and the study of evidence. The idea of intelligent design is simply not testable, and as such it cannot be a scientific theory.

Alternative theories should, and in fact often do get equal time in science classrooms and research laboratories around the world every day. Teaching a theory does not force a student to accept it as truth. Teaching a theory protect students from ignorance, educating them should they aspire to devise ways to test its validity. Science, in fact, hopes that they do, for that is precisely how society increases its knowledge of the natural world.

Science and God

Science begins not with faith, but with careful observation followed by experimentation and reasoning. Science is not whatever someone claims it to be. It is not based on anyone's beliefs or authority. Unlike faith, science can never be as untroublesome to the practitioner as believing without evidence that whatever must be so, therefore is so.

Science is a particular bunch of tools used for understanding and manipulating the physical universe. Science has, however, no tools for understanding the spiritual universe. Science's tools will never prove or disprove God's existence. For that matter, science cannot even disprove the idea of intelligent design. Science is, and only is, an explanation that best fits the data we currently have.

The theory of evolution explains life on Earth as it exists, with all its wonders, quirks and tragedies. Are there gaps? Few, but yes. But there are gaps in science everywhere. Are we to fill them all with God? The idea of intelligent design reminds me of a cartoon I once saw, in which a mathematician, struggling to complete a proof, fills the gap with the words, "And then a miracle occurs."

ID is poor science and worse theology. It reduces God to a magic word to use whenever we are stymied by a lack of information. It renders God as being everything we cannot explain. If we do not understand a natural process, it must be God's handiwork.

A majority of men and women in the sciences—be they educators, researchers or physicians—believe in a divinity. Belief in evolution can be entirely compatible with belief in God. After all, the mechanisms of creation described in Genesis 1 and 2 are left unspecified. Isn't it possible to believe that God could make life any way he wanted? Who's to say that evolution isn't the method an omnipotent God has intelligently designed to implement his elegant plan for creation?

If supporters of ID were fighting to include teaching the idea of intelligent design in comparative religion or social sciences classrooms, few would resist. Such classrooms are an excellent venue for exploring alternative versions of the origins of life. But science and faith cannot be taught alongside each other. They are different modes of knowing, different sources of wisdom.

Science and faith are not in competition. Let us not teach our children that they are.

EVALUATING THE AUTHOR'S ARGUMENTS:

In this viewpoint Todd Huffman claims that the theory of intelligent design is not science. What other author in this chapter argues from the standpoint of keeping unscientific theories out of the public school science classroom?

Chapter 3

Should Public Schools Allow Religious Activities at School?

Shown here is a model created from the bones of a child nicknamed "Lucy." At 3.3 million years old, she is thought by evolutionists to be the earliest known ancestor of humans.

Viewpoint

1

"Any prohibition of voluntary prayer in the public schools violates the right of our schoolchildren to practice their free religion, and that is not right."

Voluntary Student Prayer Should Be Protected in Public Schools

Robert C. Byrd

In the following viewpoint Robert C. Byrd argues that the First Amendment to the US Constitution protects the rights of students to engage in voluntary prayer in public schools. Byrd claims that although the Establishment Clause of the First Amendment prohibits the government from establishing religion, the courts have gone too far in using the Establishment Clause to remove religion from the schools. Byrd calls on Congress to reiterate the importance of the Free Exercise Clause of the First Amendment in protecting the rights of students to pray at school. Byrd was a Democratic member of Congress, serving in the House of Representatives and the Senate, from 1953 until his death in 2010.

Robert C. Byrd, Statement on S.J. Res. 35, 109th Congress, Senate, April 27, 2006, pp. S3719-S3721.

AS YOU READ, CONSIDER THE FOLLOWING QUESTIONS:
1. As stated by Byrd, in what year did the US Supreme Court first strike down prayer in schools?
2. In what 1984 Supreme Court case, according to Byrd, did the court claim that the Constitution does not require complete separation of church and state?
3. According to the author, what did the Supreme Court say about religious activity in public schools in *Santa Fe v. Jane Doe* (2000)?

I have long been opposed to what I call the censorship of religion in America. I have said it before. I say it again. I don't agree with many of the decisions that have come down from the courts concerning prayer in the public schools or prohibiting the display of religious items in public places. I believe in ruling after ruling some of our courts, led by the Supreme Court, have been moving closer and closer to prohibiting the free exercise of religion in America, and it chills my soul. Americans don't want religious censorship—no. Ours is a religious nation. It may not seem so but it is. We are a religious people. We may not seem so at times, not all of us, but we embrace religion as a people. We draw it close, close to us. We drape it over us, we draw it around us, we envelope our families in its protective shield. We will not shun it. We will not deny it. We will not run from it. We must be free to exercise our religious faith, if we have a religious faith, whatever it may be.

Constitutional Protection of Religion

The religion clauses of the first amendment state:

> Congress shall make no law respecting an establishment of religion, or prohibiting the free exercise thereof. . . .

In my humble opinion, too many have not given equal weight to both of these clauses. Instead, they seem to have focused only on the first clause which says "Congress shall make no law respecting an establishment of religion," at the expense of the second clause, which says, "or prohibiting the free exercise thereof."

Yes, that protects the right of Americans to worship as they please. I have always believed that this country was founded by men and women of strong faith whose intent was not to suppress religion but to ensure that the government favors no single religion over another. This principle makes a lot of sense to me; namely, that government itself should seek neither to discourage nor to promote religion. We can understand the outrage of many fine people of faith who today decry the nature of our public discourse, with its overt emphasis on sex, violence, profanity, and materialism.

In addition, we live today with the omnipresent fear of another terrorist attack, global warming, avian flu, rising fuel and health care costs, and a whole panoply of other potential calamities over which we seem to have little or no control. Our Nation has every reason to seek comfort through prayer.

Prayer in School

Nearly 44 years ago, on June 27, 1962—I was here. I was sitting over on that side of the Chamber, to my left, in the back row. Forty-four years ago, on June 27, 1962, 2 days after the U.S. Supreme Court first struck down prayer in schools, I made the following statement on the Senate floor. I said it then. I say it today.

> Thomas Jefferson expressed the will of the American majority in 1776 when he included in the Declaration of Independence the statement, "All men"—
>
> Meaning, of course, women, too—
>
> "All men are endowed by their Creator with certain unalienable rights, that among these are life, liberty, and the pursuit of happiness."
>
> Little could Mr. Jefferson suspect when he penned that line that the time would come that the Nation's highest Court might rule that a nondenominational prayer to the Creator of us all, if offered by schoolchildren in the public schools of America during class periods, would be unconstitutional. I believe this ingrained predisposition against expressions of religious or spiritual beliefs is wrongheaded,

"Honest! When I said 'Jesus Christ,'
I was *swearing*, not *praying!*"

"Honest! When I said 'Jesus Christ' I was swearing, not praying!" by Baloo Rex-May. www.cartoonstock.com.

destructive, and completely contrary to the intent of the illustrious Founders of this great Nation. Instead of ensuring freedom of religion in a nation founded in part to guarantee that basic liberty, a suffocation or strangulation, if you might, of that freedom has been the result. The rights of those who do not believe, and they are few in number who do not believe—the rights of those who do not believe in a Supreme Being have been zealously guarded to the denigration—and I repeat, denigration—of the rights of those people who do so believe.

The Supreme Court has bent over backward to prevent the government from establishing religion—which is all right—but it has not gone far enough and, in fact, our government has fallen far short of protecting the right of all Americans to exercise their religion.

The free exercise clause of the first amendment states:

Congress cannot make laws that prohibit the free exercise of religion.

Well, it seems to me that any prohibition of voluntary prayer in the public schools violates the right of our schoolchildren to practice their free religion, and that is not right. Any child should be free to pray to God of his or her own volition, whether at home, whether at church, whether at school, period.

A Constitutional Amendment

I am not a proponent of repeatedly amending the U.S. Constitution. I believe such amendments should be done only rarely and with great care. However, because I feel as strongly about this today as I have for more than 40 years, I take this opportunity, once again, as I have at least 7 times over the past 44 years, to introduce today a joint resolution to amend the Constitution to clarify the intent of the Framers with respect to voluntary prayer in schools.

Our revered Constitution—this sacred document—was conceived by the Framers neither to prohibit nor to require the recitation of voluntary prayer in public schools. Consequently, the exact language of the resolution that I am introducing to amend the Constitution simply makes that clear.

It states—get this:

Nothing in this Constitution, including any amendments to this Constitution, shall be construed to prohibit voluntary prayer or require prayer at a public school extracurricular activity.

This resolution is similar to legislation that I introduced or cosponsored starting in 1962 but more recently in 1973, 1979, 1982, 1993, 1995, and 1997.

I believe Members of the Supreme Court have placed exaggerated emphasis on the Framers' alleged intent to erect an absolute "wall of separation" between church and state. I do not share that view.

The Right to Pray

I believe the right of every schoolchild to pray or not to pray voluntarily, if he or she chooses to do so, is protected by both the free speech and the free exercise clauses of the U.S. Constitution.

Even the Supreme Court in the case of *Lynch v. Donnelly*, in 1984, agreed that the Constitution does not require the complete separation of church and state. Instead, it mandates an accommodation of all religions and forbids hostility toward any.

Let me be clear that what we are talking about is not a radical departure. It is simply a reiteration of what should already be permissible under a correct interpretation of the first amendment.

My resolution does not change the language of the first amendment, and it would not permit any school to advocate a particular religious message endorsed by the government. My resolution would simply reiterate the Framers' intent that a child should be able to utter a voluntary prayer. There is absolutely nothing unconstitutional about that.

This resolution seeks neither to advance nor to inhibit religion. It does not signify government approval of any particular religious sect or creed. It does not compel a "nonbeliever" to pray. In fact, it does not require an atheist to embrace or to adopt any religious action, belief, or expression. It does not coerce or compel anyone to do anything. And it does not foster any excessive government entanglement with religion.

This constitutional amendment is neutral. It is nondiscriminatory. It does not endorse state-sponsored school prayer. It simply allows children to pray voluntarily, if they wish to do so. It permits children to express themselves on the subject of prayer just as anyone is free to express themselves on any other topic.

The Protection of Religious Speech

As Justice [Antonin] Scalia recently held: "A priest has as much liberty to proselytize as a patriot."

The Supreme Court has held that the establishment clause is not violated so long as the government treats religious speech and other speech equally.

This resolution has a valid secular purpose, which is to ensure that religious and nonreligious speech are treated equally, and this secular purpose is preeminent. This purpose is not secondary to any religious objective.

In one of the more recent cases on the subject, the Supreme Court, in *Santa Fe v. Jane Doe* [2000], reiterated that the religious clauses of the first amendment prevent the government from "making any law respecting the establishment of religion or prohibiting the free exercise thereof." But by "no means," the Court held, "do these commands impose a prohibition on all religious activity in our public schools."

"Indeed," the Court ruled, "the common purpose of the Religious Clauses is to secure religious liberty."

Thus, Justice [John Paul] Stevens wrote:

Nothing in the Constitution as interpreted by this Court prohibits any public school student from voluntarily praying at any time before, during or after the school day.

He went on to declare, though, that "the religious liberty protected by this Constitution is abridged when the state affirmatively sponsors a particular religious practice or prayer."

So let me reiterate that the resolution I am introducing today addresses only voluntary student prayer—not state-sponsored speech.

EVALUATING THE AUTHOR'S ARGUMENTS:

In this viewpoint Robert C. Byrd argues for protection of voluntary student prayer. Does it affect the strength of his argument whether such prayer is silent or spoken aloud? Explain your answer.

Prayer Should Not Be Allowed in Public Schools

"Any and all prayer in public schools is unconstitutional, whether one form of religious ritual is used, or a virtual belief-smorgasbord is presented."

American Atheists

In the following viewpoint American Atheists argues that there should not be prayer in the public schools. The author denies that it is possible to create prayer in school that is truly voluntary and that will not offend any students. American Atheists claims that religious students have the right to pray outside of school or during their breaks. Because of the religious diversity in America, the author argues for continued separation of church and state by keeping prayer out of the public schools. American Atheists is an organization working for the civil liberties of atheists and the total, absolute, separation of government and religion.

AS YOU READ, CONSIDER THE FOLLOWING QUESTIONS:

1. According to American Atheists, which amendment to the US Constitution does school prayer violate?
2. What two religious groups do not agree on what Bible should be used, according to the author?
3. According to American Atheists, what famous American historical figure argued for the separation of church and state?

"School Prayer FAQs: What's Wrong with Prayer in Class?," www.Atheists.org. Reproduced by permission.

*Q*uestion: *What's wrong with having a short prayer in school classrooms? Surveys indicate that the majority of people favor this practice. . . .*

Answer: American Atheists opposes school prayer for a number of reasons. To begin, it is unconstitutional and a clear violation of our First Amendment. Remember, that amendment contains the "Establishment Clause" which prohibits the government from "establishing" religion. Simply put, secular institutions like the public schools should NOT be a forum for religious ritual or indoctrination.

And do a majority of people "support" school prayer? Often, those results depend on exactly how the question happens to be asked. Surveys suggest that most people reject the notion of mandatory prayer. But even if the overwhelming majority thought that prayer was, somehow, a "good idea," that does not make the practice ethically just or constitutional.

American Atheists also points out, in opposing school prayer, that prayer is not efficacious. School prayer is obviously a form of religious indoctrination; it teaches children that there are invisible, supernatural entities which can be implored and appeased through mumbling prayers or reading from holy books. . . .

Voluntary, Nonoffensive Prayer

But what about voluntary prayer? What's wrong with that?

Just how "voluntary" is it? When school authorities, including teachers organize prayer or bible recitation as part of the activities of the school day, there is clearly an element of coercion involved for students who might not wish to pray—for whatever reason. The public schools are for everyone. Having a prayer divides children into the group that prays, and the often smaller group consisting of those who do not. Experience has shown that kids who do not participate are often victims of ostracism, threats and other exclusionary practices. Is this right?

We could have a prayer that doesn't offend anyone. . . .

Really? What sort of a "prayer" would that be? Many religious groups are skeptical about organized school prayer because they fear that doctrines and prayers of other religions may be used. Catholics and Protestants have argued for decades over the issue of whose Bible should be used.

Religious Self-Identification of the US Adult Population: 1990, 2001, 2008

Religious Tradition	Estimated Number of People		
	1990	2001	2008
Total Christians	151,225,000	159,514,000	173,402,000
Other Religions	5,853,000	7,740,000	8,796,000
None	14,331,000	29,481,000	34,169,000
Don't Know/Refused	4,031,000	11,246,000	11,815,000
Total	**175,440,000**	**207,983,000**	**228,182,000**

Taken from: Barry A. Kosmin and Ariela Keysar, American Religious Identity Survey, "National Statistics on Belonging, Belief, and Behavior," Trinity College, March 2009.

Well, how about having different prayers used throughout the school year?

That idea ignores the fact that any and all prayer in public schools is unconstitutional, whether one form of religious ritual is used, or a virtual belief-smorgasbord is presented. And do you really think that different religious sects will tolerate the use of each other's prayers? Look at how pluralistic American culture has become; there are hundreds, even thousands of diverse religious beliefs. Many would clamor for "equal time" in this prayer lottery. How would Catholics react to having, say, Jewish Orthodox prayers read? What happens if a Scientologist, or Seventh-Day Adventist, or Satanist demands that prayers from those sects be used? Communities, schools, and ultimately students would become divided against each other in a religious free-for-all.

It is best to have prayer kept as a private ritual, not a public ceremony!

The Rights of Religious Students

But don't we need a Religious Equality Amendment or other legislation to protect the rights of the students who DO wish to pray?

That is not the purpose of proposed legislation such as the Religious Equality Amendment. Students can pray, even in schools, if they choose to do so. They can pray during lunch-breaks, walking or being transported to and from the school, and of course, during their free time. School prayer advocates know this; but the real purpose of the prayer-in-school movement is to either coerce everyone into joining in prayer and religious ritual, or having official government sanction of religion. That is clearly wrong, a violation of the separation of government and religion.

But I've heard about student-initiated prayer, where the students want to pray. It has nothing to do with the teachers or administrators. . . .

Before getting excited about "student initiated" prayer, ask yourself: "which students" are doing the initiating? Student populations often reflect the diversity of the culture. Some students may wish to pray in class or at official school ceremonies like graduation exercises or sporting events, but are they being fair to other students who may not wish to pray? Lately, there have been court cases involving this very question. It is clear that even in areas such as Utah where a school may have a high percentage of students from the same religious background, not all students feel comfortable with this bogus "student led" religious ritual.

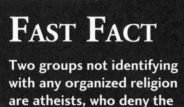

FAST FACT

Two groups not identifying with any organized religion are atheists, who deny the existence of any deities, and agnostics, who deny that we can know of such deities.

The Separation of Church and State

Our society, though, is one where most people are religious, and believers in Christianity.

Our society is, in fact, one which has over 25,000,000 individuals who consider themselves to be Atheists or non-religious in some way. Atheists comprise between 8–12% of the population. In addition to Atheists, there are millions of other Americans who are pejoratively referred to as "un-churched Americans," who rarely if ever see the need to attend regular church rituals. Religion plays only a minor role in their lives, if at all.

And consider the believers. They are fragmented into thousands of sects, denominations and different persuasions. They cannot agree on which holy book to use, which god to worship or which prayer to use. Should this problem be inflicted on the public school system? What good can possibly come from such a practice? . . .

During his presidency in the early 1800s, Thomas Jefferson wrote of the need for "a wall of separation" between state and church. To this day, scholars continue to analyze Jefferson's controversial words.

You might be right. But not having prayer in schools is a really radical idea, isn't it?

You might say that it is as American as apple pie! As advocates for the civil liberties of Atheists and other non-believers, we're in some pretty auspicious company. Thomas Jefferson, for instance, spoke of the need for a "wall of separation" between the state and the churches.

In the Virginia Statute of Religious Freedom, he insisted that no American "shall be compelled to frequent or support any religious worship, place, or ministry whatsoever. . . ." Numerous Supreme Court cases have upheld that notion, often against the fierce opposition of religious interests.

While religious events and personalities are one part of our nation's history, remember that one thing which makes America unique is the SEPARATION OF STATE AND CHURCH. It is no accident that this prohibition against the "establishment" of religion is placed in the First Amendment, along with our right to freedom of speech.

EVALUATING THE AUTHOR'S ARGUMENTS:

In this viewpoint American Atheists notes that students may pray at lunch and on their way to and from school. Would this amount of prayer satisfy the author of the previous viewpoint, Robert C. Byrd? Why or why not?

Viewpoint

3

"If we knew way back in the '60s it was wrong to force children to sit through religious activities not of their choosing, why do we decades later continue to insist on that very thing?"

Religious Holiday Activities in Schools Must Be Educational and Inclusive

Janet Pearson

In the following viewpoint Janet Pearson argues that it makes sense to limit holiday religious celebrations at public schools. Pearson contends that even though America is primarily Christian, it is not fair to the non-Christian minority to celebrate only Christian religious traditions at school. Pearson claims that guidelines from the First Amendment Center have some good suggestions that allow for some educational religious holiday activities, as long as multiple religions are included and as long as the primary purpose is informational. Pearson is associate editor at *Tulsa World*, a daily newspaper in Tulsa, Oklahoma.

Janet Pearson, "The Christmas Question: Holiday Season Raises Familiar Dispute over Religion in Schools," *Tulsa (OK) World*, November 30, 2008. Reproduced by permission.

AS YOU READ, CONSIDER THE FOLLOWING QUESTIONS:
1. In the 1960s, according to the author, what religious activities were commonplace in public school classrooms?
2. According to Pearson, how did non-Christian students deal with Christian religious holiday activities in public school in the 1960s?
3. Pearson claims that the display of religious symbols in public school is acceptable if they are used in what way?

The other day while out and about I overheard a woman grousing over the phone—actually it was impossible to avoid overhearing her—about the kids having to take part in their school's winter festival "because, you know, they can't have a Christmas festival any more."

She was clearly pretty peeved about this development, which got me wondering: What's so terrible about a winter festival?

Religious Activities at School

Of course, we all know perfectly well why the woman was displeased at the prospect of a winter festival: She obviously believes, like many other Americans, that since this is a Christian nation kids ought to be able to celebrate Christian holidays in school.

The fact there are plenty of other venues to observe one's religious beliefs isn't good enough, it seems, for some people. They want a Christmas celebration in the schools too, no matter how anyone else feels about it, and feel deprived and oppressed because schools these days won't accede to their wishes.

> **FAST FACT**
>
> Whereas Christmas, on December 25, is the most celebrated religious holiday for Christians, the holiest day for people of the Jewish faith is Yom Kippur, which occurs sometime between September 14 and October 14.

The overheard phone call took me back some 40-plus years, to when I was growing up, and Christmas events were commonplace in schools. So was the daily recitation of the Lord's Prayer, led by teachers during home-room, the beginning of the school day, and at other events. So was any number of other religious activities.

But even back during the 1960s, somebody had enough sensitivity to decide that children raised in other faith traditions ought not to have to sit through Christian activities if they didn't want to. In general, this meant Jewish children, though there may have been a few other faiths represented at the time.

The Option of Exclusion

These students were permitted to get up and leave before the Lord's Prayer, and to be absent during Christmas events and other religious holiday activities.

In the scheme of things, absenting yourself from an event likely is not the most traumatic experience a child will ever undergo. But I can still remember how uncomfortable those kids seemed when they

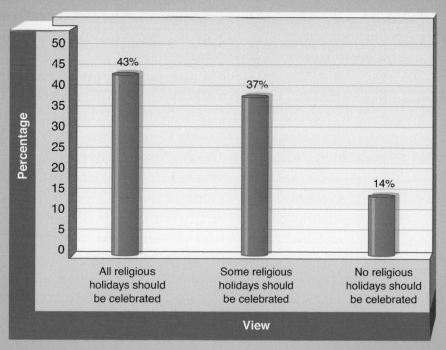

Americans' Views on Religious Holidays in Schools

Taken from: Rasmussen Reports, "Americans Still Favor Religious Symbols on Public Land, Religious Holidays in the Schools," December 10–11, 2010.

In its guidelines concerning religion in schools, the First Amendment Center suggests compromises that would allow schools to include some religious selections in holiday concerts.

scurried from the room. And I still wonder how many chose to stay and keep their faith hidden, rather than subject themselves to the discomfort caused by leaving the room.

If we knew way back in the '60s it was wrong to force children to sit through religious activities not of their choosing, why do we decades later continue to insist on that very thing?

The holiday-in-schools conflict, it turns out, does not have to be such a difficult debate. There is a middle ground that ought to be acceptable to just about all Americans. Plenty of constructive and simple advice is out there, and the celebrations can be just as joyous and festive as any from days of yore—maybe even more so.

The Middle Ground

The First Amendment Center, based at Vanderbilt University, is a nonpartisan educational and informational forum that provides guidance to the public and organizations on just such issues.

Using its guidelines, educators can devise interesting and informative holiday events, focusing "on how and when they are celebrated, their origins, histories and generally agreed-upon meanings."

Charles Haynes, a scholar at the First Amendment Center, suggests educators ask three questions in planning such events: Does it have a clear educational purpose? Will any student or parent be made to feel like an outsider by the event? Is the overall curriculum balanced and fair?

According to the center's guidelines, "If the approach is objective and sensitive, neither promoting nor inhibiting religion, this study can foster understanding and mutual respect for differences in belief."

Even the temporary display of religious symbols is permissible, if they are used as examples of cultural or religious heritage. Art, drama, music and literature with religious themes is permissible "if it serves a sound educational goal in the curriculum."

The point of any activities along these lines, center literature emphasizes, should be educational and informational—not a means of promoting any religious beliefs.

School concerts can include a variety of religious selections but may not be dominated by religious music. Dramatic productions should "emphasize the cultural aspects of the holidays." Dramas portraying the nativity scene or the Hanukkah miracle would not be appropriate.

Even when activities follow such permissible guidelines, some students still may not want to participate. In general, school leaders should allow them to choose not to attend.

To be honest, I have some pleasant memories of holiday activities in schools, as I'm sure do most of my fellow baby boomers.

Except, perhaps, my Jewish classmates, whose memories are no doubt quite different.

EVALUATING THE AUTHOR'S ARGUMENTS:

In this viewpoint Janet Pearson claims that religious holiday activities are acceptable in school if they are educational and are balanced. Give three examples of some activities that a public school might offer that meet these criteria.

Christian Religious Holidays Should Not Be Excluded from Public Life, Including Schools

"Most Americans today do not believe a manger scene or a Christmas carol in the public arena constitutes an establishment of religion."

John Eidsmoe

In the following viewpoint John Eidsmoe argues that it is a mistake to erase references to God and religion from all aspects of public life. Eidsmoe claims that there is a campaign under way to remove all Christianity from Christmas, including within public schools, public buildings, and retail stores. Eidsmoe claims that if no religious views are allowed in the public arena, religious people are treated unfairly compared with nonreligious people. Eidsmoe concludes that religious practices and symbols should be kept in the public

John Eidsmoe, "The War on Christmas," *New American*, December 22, 2008. Reproduced by permission.

realm. Eidsmoe is a professor at the Thomas Goode Jones School of Law at Faulkner University and adjunct professor at Birmingham Theological Seminary.

AS YOU READ, CONSIDER THE FOLLOWING QUESTIONS:
1. According to Eidsmoe, what are students and teachers urged to say instead of "Merry Christmas"?
2. What 1980 circuit court decision ruled that public school Christmas programs could include sacred carols, according to the author?
3. Eidsmoe says that being offended is the price we pay for what?

Because "public life" now entails virtually every part of our lives, erasing references to God entirely from public life means virtually eliminating them from America.

The War on Christmas

Imagine, if you will, a gala birthday party given in your honor. The guests will sing, dance, give presents, eat, drink, and have the merriest of times. The hitch: your name will not be mentioned, the gifts will not be for you, the celebrants won't be thinking about you, and everyone would sort of prefer that you not come.

That's all that will be left of Christmas if various groups have their way. All across the country, this year as in the past several years, there has been a concerted drive to remove all vestiges of Christianity from the celebration of Christ's birthday. For example:

- Public schools increasingly call Christmas vacation something like "winter break."
- Students and teachers are discouraged or prohibited from wishing each other "Merry Christmas," preferring "Happy Holidays" or "Seasons Greetings" instead.
- Christmas trees are either banned or called "winter trees."
- Public-school Christmas programs, er, pardon me, "winter programs," go heavy on "Frosty the Snowman" and "Deck the Halls," but the traditional Christmas carols are censored.

- Retail store employees are instructed to wish their customers "Happy Holidays" or "Seasons Greetings" rather than "Merry Christmas."
- Retail catalogs tout their goods as perfect for "the season" but avoid mentioning Christ or Christmas.
- Christmas cards, if I may call them that, wish our friends the "joys of the season" but commonly omit the "Reason for the season."
- Public buildings such as city halls, fire and police departments, etc., feature holiday displays with holly, reindeer, and candy canes, but no manger scenes and no Baby Jesus.

These practices are far from universal. But they are increasing, and they are part of a concerted drive to cleanse the public arena from any and all vestiges of America's Judeo-Christian heritage.

The Separation of Church and State
Sometimes this is done by public officials who are themselves hostile to Christianity and the Bible. But I would like to think most are motivated by other considerations.

A demonstrator stands outside a WalMart store protesting the store's use of the phrase "Happy Holidays" in place of "Merry Christmas."

Sometimes officials secularize the public arena because they don't want to offend anyone, and somehow they think they can avoid giving offense by reducing the holiday observance to the lowest common denominator. We need to remind these officials that we are offended when our heritage is stripped of its meaning. Secularism is also a belief system.

We must remember that the public sector has grown exponentially while the private sector has shrunk. Today the public arena is the main forum for the dissemination and discussion of ideas and issues: public elementary and secondary schools, public universities, public streets, public parks, public civic centers, public museums, public airwaves, and the like. The public arena has become the primary forum for the battle of ideas. If religious ideas are prohibited in the public arena but secular ideas are permitted, then religious expression and religious viewpoints are placed at a distinct disadvantage.

FAST FACT

A 2010 survey found that 69 percent of Americans prefer stores that use signs that say "Merry Christmas," whereas 24 percent preferred "Happy Holidays" instead.

Other officials naively capitulate to the argument that the First Amendment mandates an absolute separation of church and state, and therefore any and all public religious observances are unconstitutional. In fact, the federal courts have said no such thing. In *Florey v. Sioux Falls Independent School District* (1980), the 8th Circuit U.S. Court of Appeals ruled that public-school Christmas programs can include sacred carols so long as they are a balanced part of a general holiday observance. In *Lynch v. Donnelly* (1984), the Supreme Court held that a nativity scene in front of a fire station in Nantucket, Rhode Island, did not violate the First Amendment. However, in *County of Allegheny v. ACLU of Pittsburgh* (1989), the Supreme Court held 5-4 that a manger scene was unconstitutional but that a Jewish menorah did not violate the First Amendment. The court rationalized its decision by observing that the manger scene stood alone as an endorsement of Christianity, while the menorah was part of a general holiday display that included both sacred and secular symbols.

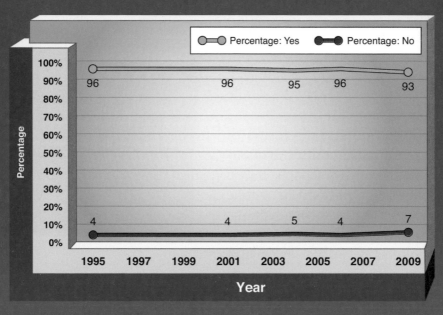

Do you celebrate Christmas?

Taken from: *USA Today*/Gallup Poll, December 12–14, 2008.

Now, almost all Americans believe in religious freedom, and hardly anyone in this country wants an established state church. But the pilgrims did not come to this country to get away from prayers at football games, and most Americans today do not believe a manger scene or a Christmas carol in the public arena constitutes an establishment of religion.

Religion in the Public Sphere

However, in recent years radical separationists have argued that a public religious practice or public display of a religious symbol endorses the religion of the majority and communicates a message to the minority that they are excluded from full participation in the life of the nation. In *Glassroth v. Moore* [M.D. Ala. 2002], the challenge to the Ten Commandments monument in the Alabama Judicial

Building was based on the fact that the plaintiffs at times had to do business in the Judicial Building, that as they walked across the rotunda they might see the monument, and that this is offensive to them. But where does the Constitution say that I will never have to see anything that offends me? I am offended by the sculpture of Themis, the Greek goddess of law and justice, that stands in front of the federal court building in Montgomery. I am offended by markers erected with my tax dollars that tell my children the Earth is billions of years old or that certain hills and valleys were formed hundreds of millions of years ago. I am offended by public use of profanity and vulgarity. But exposure to that which offends us is part of the price we pay for living in a free society.

Syndicated columnist Don Feder describes himself as "a religious Jew who wants to put Christ back in Christmas." He says, "As a lad, I was bemused by a billboard sponsored by the Knights of Columbus, which urged the public to 'Keep Christ in Christmas.' I considered the appeal superfluous, as I could not conceive of the holiday devoid of Jesus."

He adds that he's "entirely comfortable" with the concept of a Christian America, because "the morality of Christianity, though not necessarily its theology, is my morality. After all, Christians got their values from my Bible." . . .

For 2,000 years, the birth, death, and resurrection of Christ have been the central events of human history. Let us keep Christmas in our hearts, our homes, and the public square.

EVALUATING THE AUTHOR'S ARGUMENTS:

In this viewpoint John Eidsmoe argues that Christmas should be allowed to be celebrated in the public sphere. How do you think Eidsmoe and Janet Pearson, author of the previous viewpoint, would differ on how religious holidays should be celebrated at school?

Facts About Religion in Schools

Editor's note: These facts can be used in reports or papers to reinforce or add credibility when making important points or claims.

Constitutional Issues

- The Establishment Clause of the First Amendment is the portion that says, "Congress shall make no law respecting an establishment of religion."
- The US Supreme Court in *Lemon v. Kurtzman* (1971) established the three requirements laws must meet in order to be constitutional under the Establishment Clause:
  1. Laws must have a legitimate secular, or nonreligious, purpose;
  2. Laws must not have the primary effect of either advancing or inhibiting religion;
  3. Laws must not result in an "excessive government entanglement" with religion.

- The Free Exercise Clause of the First Amendment is the portion that says, "Congress shall make no law . . . prohibiting the free exercise [of religion]."
- The Supreme Court has interpreted the Free Exercise Clause as prohibiting laws that unduly restrict religious expression, while allowing government to restrict actions for which it has a compelling interest, as when the court upheld laws prohibiting polygamy in *Reynolds v. United States* (1879), despite the fact that at that time plural marriage was a religious practice of Mormons.

Public Schools

- A form of public education was in existence in the seventeenth century in the New England colonies and was largely influenced by the religious views of the Puritans and the Congregationalists.
- Private schools became the norm by the middle of the eighteenth century due to the diversity brought about by the influx of people of different religions.

- Thomas Jefferson was the first American leader to suggest creating a public school system, and his ideas helped to create the national system of formal education developed in the nineteenth century.
- Sentiments that were anti-Catholic and anti-Jewish in textbooks used in public schools led to the existence of separate Roman Catholic and Jewish schools in the mid-nineteenth century.
- During the twentieth century, the separation between church and state became more pronounced in public schools, with a prohibition on organized prayer in 1962 and a prohibition on Bible study in 1963.

Evolution, Creationism, and Intelligent Design

- *Evolution* is a theory about the origin of life that says humans evolved from other life forms over a long period of time. Charles Darwin is the scientist credited with the theory expounded in *On the Origin of Species*, published in 1859.
- *Creationism* is a theory about the origin of life that says humans were created by one or more supernatural beings. Various versions of creationism are found in many cultures and religions.
- *Intelligent design* is a theory that says there is an intelligent designer behind all creation. Though the analogy had been used in earlier centuries, William Paley is one of the most renowned authors of the theory, explained in his book *Natural Theology*, published in 1802.
- Evolution is not usually believed to be compatible with creationism. However, proponents of intelligent design sometimes believe in evolution, affirming that evolution is the grand plan of an intelligent designer.
- The intelligent designer of intelligent design theory does not necessarily have to be a god or any particular supernatural being (or even one), though many proponents in America believe a Christian god is the intelligent designer.
- A Gallup poll in 2010 revealed that 40 percent of the US population believes in creationism and 54 percent believes in evolution. Comprising the 54 percent of the population that believes in evolution, 38 percent believes evolution is guided by God and 16 percent believes evolution does not involve God.

- A Harris poll in 2009 found that 40 percent of the US population favors teaching both evolution and creationism in school, whereas 23 percent favor teaching evolution only and 17 percent favor teaching creationism only.

Prayer in Schools
- In the eighteenth, nineteenth, and early twentieth centuries, it was customary for public school to open with an oral prayer.
- The Supreme Court in *Engel v. Vitale* (1962) determined that public schools may not force students to engage in any particular prayer; however, the court has never argued that students may not engage in private, voluntary prayer.

Religion in America
According to the 2008 American Religious Identification Survey:
- Of the US population, 76 percent identifies as Christian. Among this group, however, are numerous different Christian religious traditions, including Catholic, Baptist, Methodist, Lutheran, Presbyterian, and Pentecostal, among many others.
- Of the US population, 4 percent identifies with a non-Christian religious tradition, including Judaism, Buddhism, and Islam.
- Of the US population, 15 percent identifies with no religion, which includes those who are atheist (believe there is no God), agnostic (have no beliefs about the existence or nonexistence of God) and others who identify with no religion.

Organizations to Contact

The editors have compiled the following list of organizations concerned with the issues debated in this book. The descriptions are derived from materials provided by the organizations. All have publications or information available for interested readers. The list was compiled on the date of publication of the present volume; the information provided here may change. Be aware that many organizations take several weeks or longer to respond to inquiries, so allow as much time as possible for the receipt of requested materials.

Alliance Defense Fund (ADF)
15100 N. Ninetieth St., Scottsdale, AZ 85260
(480) 444-0020 • fax: (480) 444-0028
website: www.alliancedefensefund.org

The ADF is a Christian organization that works to defend religious freedom. The organization provides legal defense for cases involving religious freedom and the sanctity of life, marriage, and the family. The ADF publishes several books, brochures, and pamphlets, including "The Truth About Student Rights."

American Atheists
PO Box 158, Cranford, NJ 07016
(908) 276-7300 • fax: (908) 276-7402
website: www.atheists.org

American Atheists is an organization that aims to protect the civil liberties of atheists, supporting absolute separation of government and religion. American Atheists holds conventions, appears in the media, and holds demonstrations in support of the separation of church and state. It publishes *American Atheist* magazine and articles such as "What Is Wrong with a Few Harmless Prayers?"

American Center for Law and Justice (ACLJ)
PO Box 90555, Washington, DC 20090-0555
(800) 296-4529
website: www.aclj.org

The ACLJ is dedicated to protecting religious and constitutional freedoms. The center has participated in numerous cases before the Supreme Court, courts of appeals, district courts, and various state courts regarding freedom of religion and freedom of speech. The ACLJ has numerous memos and position papers available at its website, including "Protecting the Rights of Students."

American Civil Liberties Union (ACLU)
125 Broad St., 18th Fl., New York, NY 10004
(212) 549-2500
e-mail: infoaclu@aclu.org • website: www.aclu.org

The ACLU is a national organization that works to defend Americans' civil rights as guaranteed in the US Constitution. The ACLU works in courts, legislatures, and communities to defend First Amendment rights, the right to equal protection, the right to due process, and the right to privacy. The ACLU publishes the semiannual newsletter *Civil Liberties Alert* as well as other publications, including "Reclaiming Our Rights: Declaration of First Amendment Rights and Grievances."

American Jewish Congress
115 E. Fifty-Seventh St., Ste. 11, New York, NY 10022
(212) 879-4500 • fax: (212) 758-1633
e-mail: contact@ajcongress.org • website: www.ajcongress.org

The American Jewish Congress is an association of Jewish Americans organized to defend Jewish interests at home and abroad. The American Jewish Congress engages in public policy advocacy—using diplomacy, legislation, and the courts—to defend religious freedom in the United States. The organization has several publications available at its website, including "Religion and the Public Schools: A Summary of the Law."

Americans United for Separation of Church and State
1301 K St. NW, Ste. 850, East Tower, Washington, DC 20005
(202) 466-3234 • fax: (202) 466-2587
e-mail: americansunited@au.org • website: www.au.org

Americans United for Separation of Church and State is a nonprofit educational organization dedicated to preserving the constitutional principle of church-state separation. The organization works to defend religious liberty in Congress and state legislatures, aiming to ensure that new legislation and policy protects church-state separation. It publishes several books and pamphlets, including *Religion in the Public Schools: A Road Map for Avoiding Lawsuits and Respecting Parents' Legal Rights.*

Becket Fund for Religious Liberty
3000 K St. NW, Ste. 220, Washington, DC 20007
(202) 955-0095 • fax: (202) 955-0090
website: www.becketfund.org

The Becket Fund for Religious Liberty is a public-interest law firm protecting the free expression of all religious traditions. The Becket Fund operates in three arenas: the courts of law (litigation), the court of public opinion (media), and in the academy (scholarship). At its website, the Becket Fund has information about cases in which it has participated, including cases aimed at protecting private religious schools from discrimination and aimed at preserving a legitimate role for religious discourse and expression in public schools.

Center for Science & Culture (CSC)
1511 Third Ave., Ste. 808, Seattle, WA 98101
(206) 292-0401
e-mail: cscinfo@discovery.org • website: www.discovery.org/csc

The CSC is a Discovery Institute program that supports research by scientists and other scholars challenging various aspects of neo-Darwinian theory and developing the theory of intelligent design. The CSC also encourages schools to focus more on weaknesses of the theory of evolution in science education. The center has numerous papers, policy positions, and videos available, including *Teaching About Evolution in the Public Schools: A Short Summary of the Law.*

First Amendment Center
1207 Eighteenthh Ave. S., Nashville, TN 37212
(615) 727-1600
e-mail: info@fac.org • website: www.fac.org

The First Amendment Center works to preserve and protect First Amendment freedoms through information and education. The center serves as a forum for the study and exploration of free-expression issues, including freedom of speech, of the press, and of religion, and the rights to assemble and to petition the government. It publishes a number of pamphlets, including *Public Schools and Religious Communities.*

First Freedom Center

1321 E. Main St., Richmond, VA 23219-3629
(804) 643-1786 • fax: (804) 644-5024
e-mail: caff@firstfreedom.org • website: www.firstfreedom.org

The First Freedom Center is a nonprofit, nondenominational, educational organization committed to advancing the fundamental human rights of freedom of religion and freedom of conscience. The center provides exhibits and programs that examine America's progress in striving for religious freedom. At its website, the center has a variety of historical religious freedom documents, as well as online exhibits related to religious freedom.

Freedom from Religion Foundation

PO Box 750, Madison, WI 53701
(608) 256-8900
e-mail: info@ffrf.org • website: www.ffrf.org

The Freedom from Religion Foundation is an educational group working for the separation of state and church. Its purposes are to promote the constitutional principle of separation of state and church and to educate the public on matters relating to nontheism. It publishes the newspaper *Freethought Today*, as well as several books and brochures such as "The Case Against School Prayer."

Foundation for Moral Law

PO Box 4086, Montgomery, AL 36103-4086
(334) 262-1245 • fax: (334) 262-1708
e-mail: info@morallaw.org • website: www.morallaw.org

The Foundation for Moral Law is a nonprofit organization that aims to restore the knowledge of God in law and government. The foundation represents individuals involved in religious liberties cases and conducts educational seminars on the importance of God in law and government. At its website, the foundation has information about cases in which it has participated, including amicus curiae (friend of the court) briefs filed in cases involving bibles in schools, a moment of silence in schools, and other issues related to students' religious rights.

Institute for Creation Research (ICR)
PO Box 59029, Dallas, TX 75229
(800) 337-0375
e-mail: info@icr.org • website: www.icr.org
The ICR works to equip believers with evidence of the Bible's accuracy and authority. The institute conducts scientific research, educational programs, and media presentations within a biblical framework. The ICR publishes *Acts & Facts*, a monthly news booklet dealing with creation, evolution, and related topics.

Intelligent Design and Evolution Awareness (IDEA) Center
PO Box 3245, Seattle, WA 98114
(858) 337-3529 • fax: (858) 569-8184
e-mail: info@ideacenter.org • website: www.ideacenter.org
The IDEA Center is a nonprofit organization dedicated to promoting intelligent design theory. The center aims to foster discussion and understanding about intelligent design theory among students, educators, churches, and other interested parties, with a primary focus of helping high school and college students form IDEA clubs to expand dialogue. It publishes many articles through its website, including *The Science Behind Intelligent Design Theory.*

Interfaith Alliance
1212 New York Ave. NW, Ste. 1250, Washington, DC 20005
(800) 510-0969 • fax: (202) 238-3301
website: www.interfaithalliance.org
The Interfaith Alliance is a national interfaith organization dedicated to protecting the integrity of both religion and democracy in America. The alliance celebrates religious freedom by championing individual rights, promoting policies that protect both religion and democracy, and uniting diverse voices to challenge extremism. It publishes a quarterly online newsletter and produces the weekly radio show *State of Belief,* with podcasts available at its website.

National Center for Science Education (NCSE)
420 Fortieth St., Ste. 2, Oakland, CA 94609-2688
(800) 290-6006 • fax: (510) 601-7204
e-mail: info@ncse.com • website: www.ncse.com

The NCSE is a nonprofit organization providing information and resources for schools, parents, and concerned citizens working to keep evolution in public school science education. The center educates the press and public about the scientific, educational, and legal aspects of the creation and evolution controversy and supplies information and advice to defend good science education at local, state, and national levels. The NCSE publishes *Reports of the National Center for Science Education*, or *RNCSE*, which gives wide coverage of all aspects of creation/evolution issues.

People for the American Way (PFAW)
2000 M St. NW, Ste. 400, Washington, DC 20036
(202) 467-4999
website: www.pfaw.org

The PFAW is an organization that fights for progressive values: equal rights, freedom of speech, religious liberty, and equal justice under the law for every American. The organization works to build and nurture communities of support for their values and to equip those communities to promote progressive policies, elect progressive candidates, and hold public officials accountable. Among its publications is the report *Back to School with the Religious Right.*

Rutherford Institute
PO Box 7482, Charlottesville, VA 22906-7482
(434) 978-3888 • fax: (434) 978-1789
e-mail: staff@rutherford.org • website: www.rutherford.org

The Rutherford Institute is a civil liberties organization that provides legal services in the defense of religious and civil liberties and aims to educate the public on important issues affecting their constitutional freedoms. The institute publishes the quarterly *Rutherford Newsletter*, the *OldSpeak* magazine, and articles including "Inside the Schoolhouse Gates: A Report on Religion in the Public Schools."

For Further Reading

Books

Boston, Rob. *Why the Religious Right Is Wrong About Separation of Church and State.* Amherst, NY: Prometheus, 2003. Traces the development of church-state relations from the Middle Ages to the modern era, explaining how the separation of church and state protects religion.

Dierenfield, Bruce J. *The Battle over School Prayer: How* Engel v. Vitale *Changed America.* Lawrence: University Press of Kansas, 2007. Explains how the first court case that addressed the constitutionality of prayer in public schools has reverberated through the subsequent decades and polarized America.

Feldman, Noah. *Divided by God: America's Church-State Problem—and What We Should Do About It.* New York: Farrar, Straus, and Giroux, 2006. Using history as a guide, proposes a solution to the church-state problem that honors religious diversity while respecting the long-held conviction that religion and state should not mix.

Gaddy, C. Welton, and Barry W. Lynn. *First Freedom First: A Citizen's Guide to Protecting Religious Liberty and the Separation of Church and State.* Boston: Beacon, 2008. Suggests ways to remind political leaders and religious communities of the importance of keeping religion and politics separate, for the sake of both institutions.

Geisler, Norman. *Creation and the Courts: Eighty Years of Conflict in the Classroom and the Courtroom.* Wheaton, IL: Crossway, 2007. Explores the testimonies and arguments of the prosecution and defense in the major court battles over creation and evolution.

Greenawalt, Kent. *Does God Belong in Public Schools?* Princeton, NJ: Princeton University Press, 2007. Concludes that the bans on school prayer and the teaching of creationism are justified, but that students should be taught more about religion.

Haynes, Charles C., Sam Chaltain, and Susan M. Glisson. *First Freedoms: A Documentary History of First Amendment Rights in America.* New York: Oxford University Press, 2006. Explores the documents that illustrate the origins and development of First Amendment freedoms in American history.

Kunzman, Robert. *Grappling with the Good: Talking About Religion and Morality in Public Schools.* Albany: State University of New York Press, 2006. Argues that public schools should help students learn how to talk about religion and morality and that students should learn to engage respectfully about diverse beliefs.

Lester, Emile. *Teaching About Religions: A Democratic Approach for Public Schools.* Ann Arbor: University of Michigan Press, 2011. Advocates an approach to teaching about religion in public schools that emphasizes respect for all views about religion and provides a special recognition of conservative Christian beliefs.

Lynn, Barry W. *Piety & Politics: The Right-Wing Assault on Religious Freedom.* New York: Three Rivers, 2007. Argues that the radicals of the religious right are attacking the constitutionally mandated separation of church and state, thereby attacking freedom of religion.

Nord, Warren A. *Does God Make a Difference? Taking Religion Seriously in Our Schools and Universities.* New York: Oxford University Press, 2010. Makes a case for requiring high school students to take a year-long course in religious studies and for discussing religion in any course that deals with religiously controversial material.

Slack, Gordy. *The Battle over the Meaning of Everything: Evolution, Intelligent Design, and a School Board in Dover, PA.* San Francisco: Jossey-Bass, 2007. Offers a firsthand account that details a battle between hard science and religious conservatives wishing to promote a new version of creationism in schools.

Solomon, Stephen D. *Ellery's Protest: How One Young Man Defied Tradition & Sparked the Battle over School Prayer.* Ann Arbor: University of Michigan Press, 2009. Tells the story of how one student's objection to mandatory school prayer and Bible reading led to one of the most controversial court cases of the twentieth century.

Thomas, R. Murray. *God in the Classroom: Religion and America's Public Schools*, Westport, CT: Praeger, 2007. Explores conflicts about religion in schools, such as the teaching of evolution, the word "God" in the pledge of allegiance, the Ten Commandments in schools, and school prayer.

Thomson, Keith Stewart. *Before Darwin: Reconciling God and Nature.* New Haven, CT: Yale University Press, 2008. Describes the rapid intensification of the challenge of scientific findings to religious beliefs during the two hundred years culminating in the publication of Charles Darwin's *On the Origin of Species* in 1859.

Periodicals and Internet Sources

American Association for the Advancement of Science. "Q & A on Evolution and Intelligent Design," 2007. www.aaas.org.

American Center for Law & Justice. "Past the Schoolhouse Gate: An Educator's Guide to Constitutionally Protected Prayer in Public Schools," May 30, 2008. www.aclj.org.

American Jewish Congress. "Religion and the Public Schools: A Summary of the Law," August 2009. www.ajcongress.org.

Americans United for Separation of Church and State. "Public School Evangelists," *Church & State*, July/August 2010.

Anthony, Alexander Orion. "An Inquiry into Intelligent Design Education," *Freethought Today*, May 2007.

Anthony, Alexander Orion. "Praying for Legal Behavior: Why Teachers Should Not Be Preachers," *Church & State*, October 2010.

Bennett, Tom, and George Foldesy. "'Our Father in Heaven': A Legal Analysis of the Recitation of the Lord's Prayer by Public School Coaches," *Clearing House*, March/April 2008.

Bookman, Jay. "Religion Better Off When Separate," *Atlanta Journal-Constitution*, October 6, 2009.

Boston, Rob. "Evolving Strategy: Creationists Promote 'Academic Freedom' Bills," *Humanist*, September/October 2008.

Campbell, Colleen Carroll. "God and the Public Schools," *Lay Witness*, September/October 2006.

Childress, Sarah. "See You in Bible Class: Georgia Plans to Teach the Good Book in Schools," *Newsweek*, May 1, 2006.

Christianity Today. "Caesar's Sectarians: The Government Keeps Trying to Favor One Kind of Religion over Another," September 2008.

Curry, Thomas. "Separation Anxiety: Church, State, and the Survival of Catholic Schools," *America*, November 22, 2010.

DeWolf, David K., and Seth L. Cooper. "Teaching About Evolution in the Public Schools: A Short Summary of the Law," Discovery Institute, June 20, 2006. www.discovery.org.

Dueck, Lorna. "Schools and Religion Do Mix," *Globe & Mail* (Toronto), April 5, 2006.

Duve, Christian de. "From the Big Bang to the Origins of Life," *Nation*, October 23, 2006.

Economist. "The Origin of Life: How Life Got Going. Maybe," February 18, 2006.

Gaddy, C. Welton. "Religious Freedom and Church-State Separation," *Human Rights*, Fall 2008.

Hardy, Dan. "Jesus Costume Banned by School Gains Some Support in Abington," *Philadelphia Inquirer*, February 25, 2007.

Haynes, Charles C. "From Battleground to Common Ground: Religion in the Public Schools Doesn't Need to Be a Flash Point for Controversy If Your District Has Crafted Policies and Exercises Them," *School Administrator*, October 2006.

Hertzke, Allen D. "The Supreme Court and Religious Liberty," *Weekly Standard*, October 18, 2010.

Jackson, Nick. "Against the Grain: 'There Are Strong Indications of Intelligent Design,'" *Independent* (London), February 8, 2007.

Leaming, Jeremy. "Illinois Decision Paved the Way for Individual Freedom," *Church & State*, February 2008.

Lebo, Lauri. "The Scopes Strategy: Creationists Try New Tactics to Promote Anti-evolutionary Teaching in Public Schools," *Scientific American*, February 28, 2011.

Liptak, Adam. "The First Amendment," *New York Times Upfront*, October 9, 2006.

Luskin, Casey. "Religion Doesn't Belong in Public Schools, but Debate over Darwinian Evolution Does," *Christian Science Monitor*, December 16, 2010.

Lynn, Barry W. "Persistently Wrong: The Religious Right Must Accept Its Losses," *Church & State*, January 2010.

Mattox, William R., Jr. "Teach the Bible? Of Course," *USA Today*, August 17, 2009.

May, Colby M. "Religion's Legal Place in the Schoolhouse," *School Administrator*, October 2006.

McCarthy, Martha. "Beyond the Wall of Separation: Church-State Concerns in Public Schools," *Phi Delta Kappan*, June 2009.

Moore, Roy. "Back to School . . . and God," *WorldNetDaily*, September 3, 2008. www.wnd.com.

Obama, Barack. "One Nation . . . Under God?," *Sojourners Magazine*, November 2006.

O'Leary, Brad. "Scrapping School Religious Holidays Solves Nothing," Townhall.com, December 25, 2010. www.townhall.com.

Omenn, Gilbert S., and Alan I. Leshner. "No Conflict Between Science and Religion," *Witchita (KS) Eagle*, July 30, 2006.

Passe, Jeff, and Lara Willox. "Teaching Religion in America's Public Schools: A Necessary Disruption," *Social Studies*, May/June 2009.

Prothero, Stephen. "It's Time to Teach Religion in Schools," *USA Today*, October 3, 2010.

Provenzo, Nicholas. "Where Science Ends and Faith Begins," *Capitalism*, January 22, 2006. www.capitalismmagazine.com.

Pyburn-Wilk, Elvia. "Intelligent Design vs. Intelligent Education," *Freethought Today*, March 2007.

Riddle, Mike. "Do You Know What Your Children Are Being Taught In School?," *Answers*, July/September 2007.

Rose, Alex. "How About a 'Freedom from Religion' in the First Amendment?," *Providence (RI) Journal*, February 3, 2010.

Russo, Charles J. "Of Baby Jesus and the Easter Bunny: Does Christianity Still Have a Place in the Educational Marketplace of Ideas in the United States?," *Education & Law Journal*, July 2006.

Van Biema, David. "The Case for Teaching the Bible," *Time*, April 2, 2007.

Waters, David. "Bible Classes in Texas Public Schools," *Washington Post*, July 25, 2008.

White, Eugene G. "The Absence of Daily Prayer," *School Administrator*, October 1, 2006.

Wilby, Peter. "Religion and Science Do Mix: Schools Need to Rethink the Curriculum," *New Statesman*, September 22, 2008.

Winder, Robert. "God, Allah or the Flying Spaghetti Monster: With Right Wing Christians on the March, Robert Winder Asks If There's Any Place for Creationism in the Classroom," *Chemistry and Industry*, January 2, 2006.

Wishingrad, Mara. "The First Amendment v. Fundamentalism: Intelligent Design in the Public School Classroom," *Freethought Today*, August 2006.

Websites

Ontario Consultants on Religious Tolerance (www.religioustoler ance.org). This website contains many articles on different religions of the world, comparative essays and opinion essays, and links to external sites involving religion.

Pew Forum on Religion and Public Life (http://pewforum.org). This website contains numerous polls and reports regarding issues at the intersection of religion and public affairs.

Teaching About Religion (www.worldvieweducation.org). This website is designed to assist history and social science teachers in handling religion in the classroom.

Index

is bad science, 42–43
prevalence of belief in, 50
scientific, public schools
   should teach, 55–61
should not be taught in
   public schools, 55–61
as world view, 64–65
See also Intelligent design
Creationists
   Cambrian explosion, rejection
      of, 42
   divergence in views of, 56–57
   tactics of, 39–40, 42–43
   theory of, studied in high
      school biology classes, *67*

D
Darwin, Charles, 50
Dawkins, Richard, *52*, 52–53
Department of Education, US,
   8
Dobzhansky, Theodosius, 43
*Doe, Santa Fe Independent
   School District v.* (2000),
   83–84
Donnelly, Lynch v. (1984),
   82–83, 99
*Dover Area School District,
   Kitzmiller v.* (2005), 72
Dover, PA school board, *71*
Dunn, Bill, 48

E
Edwards v. Aguillard (1987), 71
Eidsmoe, John, 6
Engel v. Vitale (1962), 29
Establishment Clause (First
   Amendment), 7–8, 13, 15

teaching of intelligent design
   violates, 72
Evolution
   Americans' beliefs/knowledge
      about, *42, 47*
   belief in, is compatible with
      belief in God, 76
   is not a controversial theory
      among scientists, 73, 75
   is ongoing, 59–60
   many scientists are skeptical
      of, 47
   public schools should teach
      criticism of, 44–48
   theory of, studied in high
      school biology classes, *67*
   without alternatives should
      be taught in public schools,
      38–43
Expelled (film), 52, 53

F
Feder, Don, 101
First Amendment
   religion clauses of, 79
   See also Establishment Clause;
      Free Exercise Clause
First Amendment Center,
   94–95
*Florey v. Sioux Falls Independent
   School District* (1980), 99
Fossil record
   of Cambrian explosion, 42
   consistency in, 57–59
   creationists reject, 42, 64
   is evidence of evolution, 73
Fowler, David, 44
Free Exercise Clause (First
   Amendment), 7, 8, 81–82

Picture Credits

AP Images, 45
AP Images/Carolyn Kaster, 71
AP Images AJ Mast, 10
AP Images/Daniel Shanken, 40
AP Images/Rick Smith, 65
AP Images/Akira Suemori, 52
AP Images/Max Whittaker, 98
© BMD Images/Alamy, 28
Gale/Cengage Learning, 14, 24, 35, 42, 47, 51, 67, 74, 87, 93, 100
Lawrence Migdale/Photo Researchers, Inc., 94
© Myrleen Pearson/Alamy, 33
© Adrian Sherratt/Alamy, 16
© Don Smith/Alamy, 37
Volker Steger/Photo Researchers, Inc., 77
© SuperStock/SuperStock, 89

PCHS Media Center
Grant, Nebraska